THE RENAISSANCE IMAGE OF MAN AND THE WORLD

THE RENAISSANCE IMAGE

of

MAN AND THE WORLD

Edited by

Bernard O'Kelly

Ohio
State
University
Press

EDITOR'S FOREWORD

THE PAPERS that constitute this volume (apart from the Introduction) were read at the Fourth Annual Conference on the Humanities sponsored by the Graduate School of Ohio State University under the same title as the volume, October 27 and 28, 1961.

In addition to the papers, the conference included a panel discussion led by Professor Josephine Bennett, of Hunter College; a program of Renaissance dancing directed by Professor Helen Alkire and Mrs. Katherine Wyly, with music under the direction of Professor Herbert Livingston, all of Ohio State University; an exhibit of Renaissance books and manuscripts, sponsored by the Ohio State University Library; an exhibit of Renaissance graphic works and a general exhibit of Renaissance art, under the direction of Professor Anthony Melnikas of Ohio State University, with the co-operation of Mr. Mahonri Young, Director of the Columbus Gallery of Fine Arts; and a program of Renaissance music by the New York Pro Musica, under the direction of Noah Greenberg.

Special consultants to the conference were Professor Madeleine Doran, University of Wisconsin; Noah Greenberg; and Professors Marvin Eisenberg, University of Michigan; Wallace K. Ferguson, University of Western Ontario; Glen Haydon, University of North Carolina; Charles Mullett, University of Missouri; Charles Parkhurst, Oberlin College; Palmer Throop, University of Michigan; and A. S. P. Woodhouse, University of Toronto.

The editor wishes to express his personal gratitude to all these persons, and to Professors Franklin Pegues, Harold Grimm, Ruth Hughey, Joan Webber, Frank Ludden (all of Ohio State University); Professor Vern Torczon of Louisiana State University, New Orleans; and the countless others who made possible the conference and, indirectly, this volume. He wishes also to thank his wife, Marcia O'Kelly, for her work in preparing the Index. Above all, he wishes to thank in this permanent form Vice-President Everett Walters of Boston University, formerly Dean of the Graduate School at Ohio State University, the originator and unsparing supporter of the Humanities Conferences.

CONTENTS

Introduction
  Bernard O'Kelly   3

Philosophy and Humanism in Renaissance Perspective
  Paul Oskar Kristeller   29

The Renaissance: The Literary Climate
  Douglas Bush   53

The Image of Man in Renaissance Art:
From Donatello to Michelangelo
  H. W. Janson   77

Paolo Toscanelli and His Friends
  Giorgio de Santillana   105

Music of the Renaissance
as Viewed by Renaissance Musicians
  Edward E. Lowinsky   129

Notes on the Contributors   178

Index   181

ILLUSTRATIONS

(following page 86)

Fig. 1.—Giovanni Pisano. "Virtue." Detail of the marble pulpit, Pisa Cathedral. 1302–10.   Plate   I

Fig. 2.—Donatello. Bronze "David." Museo Nazionale, Florence. *ca.* 1430–32.   Plate   I

Fig. 3.—Nanni di Banco. "Isaiah." Florence Cathedral. 1408.   Plate   II

Fig. 4.—Donatello. Marble "David." Museo Nazionale, Florence. 1408; modified 1416.   Plate   II

Fig. 5.—Donatello. "St. Mark." Or San Michele, Florence. 1411–13.   Plate   III

Fig. 6.—Taddeo Gaddi. "David." Baroncelli Chapel, S. Croce, Florence. *ca.* 1330–35.   Plate   III

Fig. 7.—Michelangelo. "David." Accademia, Florence. 1501–4.   Plate   IV

Fig. 8.—Donatello. "St. George." Museo Nazionale, Florence. *ca.* 1416.   Plate   IV

Fig. 9.—Nanni di Banco. "Four Saints" ("Quattro Coronati"). Or San Michele, Florence. *ca.* 1410–14.   Plate   V

Fig. 10.—Donatello. "Beardless Prophet." Museo dell'Opera del Duomo, Florence. 1416–18.   Plate   VI

Fig. 11.—Donatello. "Bearded Prophet." Museo dell'Opera del Duomo, Florence. 1418–20.   Plate   VI

Fig. 12.—Donatello. "Prophet" ("Zuccone"). Museo dell'Opera del Duomo, Florence. 1423–25.   Plate   VII

Fig. 13.—Donatello. Prophet ("Jeremiah"). Museo dell'Opera del Duomo, Florence. 1427–35.   Plate   VII

Fig. 14.—Florence Cathedral, detail from Andrea da Firenze, "The Church Militant and Triumphant." Spanish Chapel, S. Maria Novella, Florence. 1365–68.   Plate VIII

Fig. 15.—Detail of Fig. 10.   Plate   IX

Fig. 16.—Roman portrait. Museo Vaticano, Rome. *ca.* 50 B.C.   Plate   IX

Fig. 17.—Detail of Fig. 12.   Plate   X

Fig. 18.—So-called "Trajanus Decius." Museo Capitolino, Rome. Third century A.D.   Plate   X

Fig. 19.—Detail of Fig. 13.   Plate   XI

Fig. 20.—Detail of Fig. 2.   Plate   XII

Fig. 21.—"Head of Antinous." Museo Archeologico, Florence. *ca.* 125 A.D.   Plate XIII

Fig. 22.—Donatello. "Angel with Tambourine." Staatliche Museen, Berlin-Dahlem. 1429.   Plate XIV

Fig. 23.—Michelangelo. "David." Pen drawing, Cabinet des Dessins, Louvre, Paris. 1501.   Plate XIV

Fig. 24.—Bernardo Rossellino. Tomb of Leonardo Bruni. S. Croce, Florence. *ca.* 1445–50.   Plate XV

Fig. 25.—Doorway of the Pantheon, Rome. *ca.* 115–25 A.D.   Plate XVI

INTRODUCTION

INTRODUCTION

By

Bernard O'Kelly

GEORGE GASCOIGNE urged the priests to pray for "such as be historiographers" that they "trust not too much in every tattling tongue,/ Nor blinded be by partiality," and those professionally concerned with the Renaissance have needed this *deprecatio periculorum*—and still need it—as much as anyone. The attempt to understand any past is, of course, chancy at best: most people probably notice that even their own past is not always available on demand. Time is a cruel banker, as Ralegh says, taking in trust our all we have, and paying us but with age and dust. We cannot know with certainty exactly how we felt ten years ago— or yesterday—and often we do not really want to. Apart from misremembering things done and said, we simply do not have the imaginative power to relive the actual circumstances—always infinitely complex—of any past moment or minute or hour. We recall most vividly, I suppose, intense and simple things, experiences somehow concentrated and free from seriously relevant distractions; and consequently, we like sometimes to pretend that most of our own past (or of some larger past—the Renaissance, say) had that kind of simplicity and concentration and completeness when it didn't.

To rediscover the past, we use records, written or other. Whether or not these are conceived as art, they always do to some extent what art does: they give the present some kind of permanence or immortality, an armor against time. And the present needs it—

> . . . Ere a man hath power to say "Behold!"
> The jaws of darkness do devour it up.
> So quick bright things come to confusion.

Lysander is right to extend his pleasantly poignant bombast concerning the perilously fugitive quality of things beyond his primary subject, love, to all human experience, or at least to all things that are truly bright and alive. Men have little power against time; and when they die, there is more truth than nostalgia in the words of Ecclesiastes: "For the memory of them is forgotten. Also their love, and their hatred, and their envy, is now perished; neither have they any more a portion for ever in any thing that is done under the sun." Among others, the artist and the scientist, the chronicler, the poet, the philosopher, and the composer all decline (in any age) the advice that follows in Ecclesiastes simply to eat, drink, and be merry, and instead strive in their various ways to rescue the present—or a present—from oblivion, from the chaos that is perpetual loss. During the Renaissance many people were unusually concerned to catch and fix the present, the here-and-now intersection of time and space that had never been before and would never be again. In this may lie some part of an explanation at once for the enduring vigor of their artistic and

hard to understand

intellectual enterprises and for their determination to recover the past. Their literature frequently shows this preoccupation; Samuel Daniel's lines present a common theme uncommonly well:

> O blessed Letters, that combine in one
>   All ages past, and make one live with all,
>   By you we do confer with who are gone,
>   And the dead-living unto counsel call;
>   By you th'unborn shall have communion
>   Of what we feel, and what doth us befall.
> Soul of the world, Knowledge, without thee
>   What hath the earth that truly glorious is?
>   Why should our pride make such a stir to be,
>   To be forgot?

This heightened consciousness of time, the intellectual habit of locating oneself and one's present at the juncture of a defined past and a projected future (both much larger than one's own lifespan) carries with it a consequence very important to the future historiographer. (I am using the term here, it will be apparent, not of professional historians, but of all those who seek to know, understand, and appreciate the works and ways of the past.) When a man makes time past and time to come primary terms of his own self-definition and keys to the importance both of his being and of his works, time will truly be of the essence of what he creates or in any way projects from himself. The concern itself to build a monument more lasting than bronze will not normally exist when there is no informed interest in the monuments of men long dead and no optimistic respect for the opinion of men yet unborn; the desire to make one's age great—"to do worthy the writing, and to write/ Worthy the reading"—presupposes an awareness at once of the otherness of one's own age and of its place in a continuing succession of ages. Centuries later, we can and do find the works and days of the Renaissance the more vivid and the more communicative precisely because they were in their own time conceived as having, and indeed were effectively endowed with, relevance and significance for time in both its reaches. Quite apart, then, from the actual volume of extant records and relics, the Renaissance seems eminently to offer itself to our concern and our understanding because Renaissance men and women—many of them, at least—habitually and efficaciously had in mind the hope that future generations would have communion of what they felt and what befell them, and would judge these worthy of the fine precedents of antiquity which they labored to recover and preserve.

As Professor de Santillana points out in his paper in this volume, we do not have much direct evidence about Paolo Toscanelli; but we can know rather a great deal about him and can conjecture even more with some degree of safety. Our scope in this respect depends, I believe, to a large extent on Toscanelli's own attitude and that of his contemporaries toward time and the importance within it of their thoughts and deeds. The very concept of periodization, as we now understand and practice it, is (for better or for worse) one of our legacies from men and women of the Renaissance. They may have used the device crudely and without much consistency, even by our own unexacting standards, but its importance to them demonstrates their desire to cope with the reality of time and change and to establish over that reality some degree of intellectual mastery. Perhaps the one thing that could not have been subtracted

(6)

(without destroying the unity of the rest) from the authentic and basic cultural community in the Renaissance of which Professor Bush writes convincingly is the set of assumptions and preoccupations characterizing the age in the matter of man's situation in time. Certainly the cultural awareness of themselves that people had in the Renaissance was inextricably and importantly bound up with their sense of time and of themselves as somehow definable in time. For this, as I have indicated, we have every reason to be grateful.

Unfortunately, even with special help from the peculiar awareness of time that existed in the Renaissance, we are always in peril of unsuspected ambush by ancient enemies that can subvert or distort our conceptions of the past. There are more partialities than the one Gascoigne wanted the priests to deprecate, and I should like to review some of them here, especially since the essays that follow demonstrate, each in its own way, how one may make efficacious the prayer urged by Gascoigne.

Among the partialities that can blind us to truth about the past, the most perverse and perhaps the most insidious is precisely the desire for absolute clarity of vision, for simplicity, for complete definition. The tendency in this direction is, I have suggested, always a companion of human thought about the past, and the metaphoric name "Renaissance" itself offers a special invitation to the mind's instinct for univocal definition, since it implies the unity of a single—if prolonged—event. Further, the Renaissance has been customarily looked upon as the beginning of "modern times," so that the quest for knowledge of it translates itself easily into a search for some single core of meaningfulness for ourselves, and the real kinds of significant homogeneity that did exist within the Renaissance, especially in comparison with our own time, can make that search both promising and enticing.

⟨ The partiality for simplicity and neatness, then, may make us overeager to know when the Renaissance began, within a year or two, a decade or two, and when it ended: we would like our periodization in sharp focus.⟩We may become impatient to discover the three essential achievements of the Renaissance, or the five infallible tests of the true Renaissance spirit, or the eleven fundamental preoccupations and attitudes of Renaissance man, seeking to reduce God's plenty (or man's variety) to common denominators that are too low⟩ For monistic minds there will always be the "one great central fact about the Renaissance"; and since thousands of such minds have been at work, there are in some sort of currency thousands of "one great central facts" about the Renaissance. As soon as a man accepts one of these as final, his mind is largely relieved of the burden of complexity, of diversity, of change, paradox, and inconsistency—eternal companions of human existence. Dualistically inclined minds produce perhaps more dangerous packages, because these seem more sophisticated and carry an intrinsic, a formal, plausibility. "There are two main currents in the Renaissance." Yes, and so many pairs of candidates have been proposed in elaborations of some such statement that simply to collect and document them might now prove a life's work. There seems to be, indeed, some mysterious cause—although perhaps it is nothing more mysterious than the circumstance that many Renaissance minds were themselves inclined to dualism—making the Renaissance more prone to dichotomistic treatment than any other area of study: we are often invited now to divide not only the Renaissance but

(8)

Renaissance scholars as well into two currents or two conflicting camps, and the choices offered for the exercise seem well on their way to becoming legion in their turn, although they always seem to come in matched pairs.

It is not, of course, that the great central facts and the significant polarities about the Renaissance are not usually true and important, especially if one abstracts from the exclusive claims for truth and importance made on their behalf. Obviously, too, many of them are presented as heuristic or didactic devices by means of which we may organize our knowledge, and nothing more. The danger lies in settling with too much finality upon one or two (or five or eleven) significant keys to the understanding of the Renaissance and then trying to make all the doors fit the keys. Partiality of this kind makes us more inclined to dismantle facts than to dismantle schemata.

The chief antidote to the mind's partiality for reducing complexities to oversimplifications lies in the recognition that the quest for truth must always be a quest for truths. There is no Truth about the Renaissance—there are truths, an almost infinite number of them, and some of them ought to seem to us very strange bedfellows indeed. The student of the Renaissance should see himself, not as the Redcrosse Knight setting out to right the wrongs of Una and see her face unveiled, but in the much less heroic role of a juggler learning to keep constantly more and more items before his eyes without dropping any or allowing their number—however great—to obscure for him the existence among them of relationships and patterns. The Redcrosse Knight, after all, discovers that there are a thousand more things in the world than Una and a dragon, and that they are all important, however unforeseen they may be, or however confusing.

A second historic obstacle to a true understanding of the Renaissance has lain in the apparently natural tendency of the human mind to approximate human history, human experience in the past, to a single life process. The "organic metaphor" has been under attack from many quarters for a long time, but its strength is as the strength of ten: men continue to discover the seeds and roots of the Renaissance, its first tender shoots, the growing saplings; they observe and point out a flowering, a maturity, the lasting fruits, the decay. This partiality can be worse than the first, since it imposes a preconceived conceptual structure on human thought and events instead of simply deducing one a posteriori. It seems necessary to remind ourselves frequently that human history is not a magnolia tree or a rosebush, and that analogies intended to clarify reality can and must obscure reality when they are allowed to approach literalness. I might add that for certain obvious reasons the Renaissance entices some men to organize their thoughts in a solar instead of an organic allegory: dawn, daybreak, high noon, twilight, and sunset take on for them a peculiar validity that we do not usually accord metaphors, with the particular harm in this instance that one is led half-consciously to conceive of the time just before (and just after) the Renaissance as night.

A third partiality with widespread bad results for the understanding of the Renaissance might be called the partisan or ideological bias. The militant secularist, the doctrinaire anticlerical, will labor to establish (if he doesn't simply assume) that everyone and everything of any importance during the Renaissance tended to liberate man or assert his freedom from ecclesiastical authority and institutional religion in general: he will find all the glory and splendor of the age to lie in man's emancipation from the darkness of superstition and the shackles of theistic orthodoxy. The sectarian Catholic, similarly, will find ways to interpret all the major achievements of the Renaissance so that they redound to the credit of the Church: finding Erasmus distinctly non-sectarian (and consequently a good deal more Catholic than himself), he may relegate him to a historical limbo; he may spend much time and energy trying to diminish or obscure the unlovely aspects of the Renaissance papacy; he may even comb Shakespeare's plays, not for their better understanding or appreciation, but for evidence (which he will not find) or hints that their author was a crypto-Catholic. The scholar who espouses eccentricity will show that the Renaissance above all else prized singularity, originality, and non-conformism; the traditionalist will demonstrate that love of tradition and fear of disorder are the motivating forces in Renaissance artistic and intellectual activities. The proponent of free-enterprise capitalism interprets the Renaissance as an age of great progress occasioned by resolute economic privatism (and privateering); the moralizing collectivist relates all major aspects of the age to its strong sense of community and its elevation of human values over those related to economics and power. The aestheticist and the humanist; the atheist, the agnostic, and the believer; the rationalist and the anti-rationalist—men and women of all these and of hundreds of other more or less successfully systematized preconceptions at one time or another have seen the real significance of the Renaissance to lie in its having been lucky enough to share their preoccupations and convictions. Sometimes, of course, a partisan bias in scholarship owes its origin to nothing other than a man's having "rasshelye . . . spoken that cummeth fyrste to hys tonges ende," and afterwards feeling obliged to "studye for reasons wherewyth to defende and confyrme hys fyrste folyshe sentence."

In passing, it may be remarked that one kind of partisanship may be disappearing from contemporary scholarship, although its effects will endure for a long time: renascentiolatry. Just as the humanists reinvented periodization, adopting it in the main from their models in the Augustan age, so they reinvented the Augustan device of almost worshiping—or pretending almost to worship—the men and ways of an earlier age. This legacy was in turn gratefully accepted by many nineteenth-century men and women, "Romantics" and others, especially if they were admirers of the good life but abhorrers of the means provided by the Industrial Revolution for achieving it. They turned to the Renaissance with devotion; and instead of equipping Plato with vigil lamps and a halo, they decked out the entire age with these candescent but not always illuminating marks of glory. For them the good was the Renaissance, the non-Renaissance was the bad. The lamps have not all been extinguished, but it is harder for us—partly because we cannot think of human history (or human nature) in quite the same numinous way—to mythologize or sanctify the Renaissance. In this loss to devotion, there can be, I think, only gain for truth.

Partisan scholarship of any sort should not, of course, be condemned without full recognition that it has its beneficial side effects. The reading of many conflicting partisans, while it may result in a rich and desperate muddle for the mind, may also happily leave one with a balanced eclectic view. Moreover, even the most partial scholars can deserve our gratitude for the industry with which they dig for evidence to support their diversified investments. The evidence is always valuable, even when the conclusions it was meant to support must be committed to an eccentrics' paradise.

Closely related to partisanship, one may discern a fourth peril to true understanding, a trick of perspective which is less easily taken into account and corrected. No matter how loyally he tries to be something other, every man who retains some shreds of sanity must remain a child of his own time. And it is of the nature of our minds to treat the past as being most importantly a preparation or an overture to the present we live in, since that is (naturally) what is most important and most real to us. Because of this tendency, we show a warm interest in those Renaissance things and people that seem most relevant, most congenial, to our own time and experience, but play at best the role of antiquarians with regard to those things our ancestors said and thought and did which men have subsequently discarded as old-fashioned, unworthy, or based on false scientific assumptions. To what we find sympathetic in the Renaissance, undue emphasis can easily accrue by means of a kind of massive, collective egocentricity: a search for ourselves in others. The phenomenon was not unfamiliar to men in the fifteenth and sixteenth centuries; the pre-anthropologists and proto-ethnologists among the discoverers and explorers were delighted at the recognition of familiar ways and concepts in people of alien cultures, and not infrequently misunderstood what they met because of an eagerness to confirm the essential oneness, as they understood it, of mankind. There is also a perversely topsy-turvy version of this partiality: a morbid and exaggerating fascination with whatever in the other culture or age makes it markedly different from one's own, whatever startles or titillates by its otherness from one's own experience. In the "world" of the early travel books "nothynge is more easye to be founde, then be barking Scyllaes, rauenyng Celenes, and

Lestrygones deuowerers of people, and suche lyke greate and vncredyble monsters." Some scholars seem to have approached the Renaissance with a determination to find similar marvels.

Perhaps more often, however, fables—whether monstrous or not—persist in Renaissance scholarship simply because real knowledge is lacking. The reader will observe more than once in the papers that compose this volume, and in much contemporary Renaissance scholarship elsewhere, the phrase "the present state of our knowledge"; many of the errors and false emphases of past research have come from insufficient awareness of the inadequacy, not of any one scholar's information, but of the information collectively held and available to anyone. One of the greatest contributions that can now be made to Renaissance studies lies in the precise location of our ignorance and the discerning of what significant information needs to be discovered or collected. Apart from giving direction to profitable research, this permits us at least to make allowance for what we do not know.

Finally—not that I intend here an exhaustive syllabus of perils—there is a kind of partiality in language itself. In seeking to know the Renaissance, we must depend, as I have said, on written records, and this is true even when our immediate concern is with non-linguistic art forms such as music, sculpture, painting, and architecture (see Professor Lowinsky's and Professor Janson's papers below). Words are dangerous, however. It is true that language has, in some of its uses, a peculiar toughness and durability: "stark naked" remains connotatively powerful for us long after we have forgotten that "stark" in this phrase means "rump" (although linguistically sophisticated birdwatchers might recognize the root from the name of the redstart). But the resiliency of language is not always of direct help to us, as this perhaps extreme example shows, and language accepted uncritically must be recognized as a tortuous or haphazard road to knowledge: someone from an earlier age would know what we meant by "stark naked" or "redstart," but might well be astonished to hear that a play had involved "stark" acting. Time and change play silent games with our words. When we meet in fifteenth- and sixteenth-century authors words that we have reason to know we don't understand, we set about finding out what they meant. Used literally or figuratively, words related to psychological assumptions, for instance, or to medical practice or physical science, are fairly easy to deal with: element, humor, complexion, melancholy, spirit, fantasy, animal—these and hundreds of words like them we now, thanks to the work of many scholars, make an adjustment for in our minds when we have begun to move about in Renaissance texts. No contemporary sense, we are fully aware, will be quite adequate for such words. But we can and perhaps must fall into traps with words for which we habitually make no adjustment. No matter how hard we try, we can never now be able to hear quite what our ancestors heard in "fire," "water," "earth," or "air"; and however alert we may be to the concept of elements in Renaissance thought, we are not likely to be very sensitive, habitually, to the individual names of the elements. The more familiar and basic the word, the more likely we are to go wrong. It is, I think, virtually impossible for us to know what "the dark" or "darkness" was for people who had only fire to supplement the sun, moon, and stars; and we can't really know what "light" was for them, either. Part of what they understood by "day" and "night" is similarly inaccessible to us, because we cannot erase our own consciousness of man's victory over physical darkness, and consequently much of their most meaningful symbolism reaches us only secondhand and in an approximate form.

Gentle, fair, wild, sweet, mountainous, old, distance, savage, foreigner, generous, beer, afar: hundreds of important and unimportant "ordinary" words are at least minor traps for us when we read Renaissance texts, carrying meanings for our ancestors that we can scarcely imagine, and too rarely try to imagine.

Moreover, as Professor Kristeller points out in his paper in this volume, we use words and categories of thought in talking about the Renaissance that people alive then did not have, or for which they had contents different from ours. A constant check on our use of language is of the greatest importance in all study of the past; but in our study of the Renaissance the check is all the more necessary because the "modern" European vernaculars were then taking—or had taken relatively recently— the form which, by and large, they have kept to our day. We are less likely to make mistakes reading vernacular documents of earlier ages, in which the more obvious differences from our own usage can of themselves impose upon us a warier sensitivity to the perils of language.

{ Oversimplification, partisanship, the imposing of metaphor upon reality, the distorting effects of time, inadequate knowledge, a too unsophisticated use of language—all of these have had particular ways of causing writers since the Renaissance to present an image of the age that belies to some extent the reality, and it is usually with relief and often with surprise that one turns from the partialities of later "historiographers" to the firsthand reports of people who lived in the age itself. } One must be on guard, of course, against the possibility of an obvious (but rather subtle) fallacy in the formulation of some such principle as "the true understanding of the Renaissance is to be found, not in the schematizations and structured conceptualizations of later men and women, but in the firsthand understanding of it that belonged to men and women who actually lived during the Renaissance"; on the other hand, if one is seeking the reality of the Renaissance, clearly one must always begin and end with the direct testimony of the only human beings who were on-the-spot witnesses.

The scholar does not thereby escape either the disadvantages or the uncertainties of periodization; in a sense, as I have said, the Renaissance must take a large part of the credit or the blame for the importance to our thought of this uncertain and dubious science. The fifteenth- and sixteenth-century practitioners were, if anything, less unanimous, less careful about the bases of their divisions, and more capricious in assigning *termini a quo* and *ad quem* for past ages and for their own age, "modern times," than scholars are likely to be now. But Gascoigne can remind us that scholars must guard against tattling tongues as well as partiality. Taking his words again in a large sense, we should recall that witnesses in any age or circumstance are to be credited not as to what is true, but (other things being equal) as to what they believe to be true. And the concern of this volume is precisely that: the things that Renaissance men and women believed to be true of themselves. We have no right, in any event, to be disappointed at the discovery in their testimony of contradiction and inconsistency; even in this age of flourishing social sciences, men and human events still resist rigid classification and precise definition. Roger Ascham is typical (at least of the English scene) when he writes in one place of the sad condition in his "forefathers' time, when papistry, as a standing pool, covered and overflowed all England"; and he is equally representative when he writes—without, one must imagine, any awareness of a possible inconsistency— that his country should return to its "old wont" and find in following the same forefathers' example "labor, honest pastime, and virtue" so that the youth will be "plucked from idleness, unthrifty games, and vice." The "new" age, mainly a bad thing, seems for Ascham (here) to have begun when Englishmen put down their longbows for reasons other than eating, sleeping, or praying. Elsewhere he seems to see the new age, insofar as it is a good thing, beginning with England's emancipation from Rome, and insofar as it is bad, beginning with the "new" phe- nomenon of Italianate Englishmen and the organized attempt by Catholics to destroy English moral fiber by promoting obscene literature. Stephen Gosson, in a famous passage, goes so far as to exhort his readers to find again the qualities of "Englishmen" of the second century (although one may suspect hyperbole in a few of the virtues he notes, like going naked and standing dinnerless up to the chin in marshes for several days), and seems to situate the beginning of all modernity— that is, all degeneracy—with the new popularity of the "secular" theater. Others in the time, taking a more academic view, dated the new age from the return of Greek studies to western Euro- pean universities, or the end of Aristotelian scholasticism and the substitution of a newly recovered Platonism. Platonism had, of course, never been lost, and, as Professor Kristeller reminds us in this volume and elsewhere, Aristotelianism did not leave the universities.

The examples of Ascham and Gosson remind us that particular perils lurk in English testimony about the Renais- sance. The Tudor usurpation, together with accompanying administrative changes and (until our own time) perhaps history's most successfully engineered collective brain-washing about the immediate past, provided most people, it would appear, with a ready-made watershed, so that in later times what had happened before Bosworth Field had to seem somehow much more remote than what happened afterward. Within a few decades, the Reformation, in England a series of events in which four Tudor monarchs were very closely involved, confirmed the sense of difference from the past. As a result, even now in the minds of many, "Tudor," "Reformation," and "Renaissance" are concepts so closely linked—or so richly muddled—as to be virtually synonymous; and much intellectual energy and resourcefulness that might have been better spent has gone into endless elaborations of allegedly significant noncasual relationships among the three. The near-coincidence of the introduction into England of printing presses may have seemed to sixteenth-century Englishmen another aspect of the "Tudor" age. Almost inescapably, too, the new western and African explorations of the late fifteenth and the sixteenth centuries were closely bound up in contemporary English minds —and more than chronologically—with the Tudor dynasty; through the reigns of the first four Tudors, especially, and even in that of the last, with misgivings in the more farsighted of those minds because the English weren't keeping up with the Spanish and Portuguese. These two further associations—part of the habitual thinking (or non-thinking habit) of that time— have left their mark in later generations. One sometimes gets the impression from writers in the tradition of the English language that Richard III or his son could not have commissioned the Cabots or even that with a Plantagenet ruling in England, Columbus, Magellan, and Juan Ponce de Leon would have spent their days idly reading *Amadis of Gaul* and then died unknown in the Middle Ages. The patronage extended to Caxton by two Plantagenet monarchs is overlooked. The confusion—then and now—has extended so far as to make the institution of a Greek readership at Cambridge in Henry VIII's reign causally relevant to the Oath of Supremacy and the Thirty-Nine Articles, and then to assume that these in turn are somehow contributing causal elements in the genius of Marlowe and Shakespeare.

Shakespeare himself, however, although he accepted for dramatic purposes much of the official Tudor vilification of Richard III and celebrated, indirectly at least, the Tudor new age, was less susceptible than many to the false time-sense occasioned in England by the rough chronological coincidence of New Learning, Tudors, printing, American discoveries, and the Protestant reform. The watershed in Shakespeare's historical plays, insofar as there is one, is rather the time of Chaucer. Critics used to find the chief difference between the tone of *I* and *II Henry IV* and *Henry V,* on the one hand, and *Richard II,* on the other, in a reassuring schema of Shakespeare's evolving art: one can still find editors who urge their readers to notice the development of his dramatic craft from a certain ceremonial stiffness or formality in *Richard II* to the vitality or liveliness of *I Henry IV,* as though we could be sure that the tone or atmosphere of the former play would have been substantially changed if Shakespeare had known better, i.e., if he had written it three or four years later. The stage has, I suspect, always provided the refutation of this view: *Richard II* is as alive as the best of Shakespeare's plays. Its world, the atmosphere in which its action takes place, is simply not the modern world as Shakespeare knew it. It is, of course, closer to and more like Shakespeare's modern world than that of *Macbeth, Julius*

Caesar, or (above all) *King Lear;* but Richard's death at Pomfret seems to carry symbolically the weight of the death of an age, and Bolingbroke's usurpation initiates a new and a not altogether amiable time. The ancient sacred kingship is ended; in the conflict between loyalty and expediency, loyalty's claims are henceforth muddy and muddled, and are based on abstractions and projections (like nations, countries, and "parties") rather than on relationships or symbols. One facet of the new man, the Renaissance *homo politicus,* finds its second-best English incarnation in Henry IV, who sacrifices everything except prudence to expediency—its best is Shakespeare's Henry V, who saves certain superficial human graces and certain personal eccentricities as well as prudence from the holocaust of relationship to practical ambition and achievement.

The time of Chaucer and Wycliffe, of John Ball and Wat Tyler, might indeed be seen as a more likely beginning of a new age in England than that of Colet, Erasmus, and Skelton. If there is some valid sense in which one can view Henry IV as a typical Renaissance prince displacing the last "medieval" monarch to rely (ineffectually) on a stable, feudally structured society, surely there are many senses in which Chaucer may be said to be the first English Renaissance poet. It is he, really, who gives us the picture of the last knight in Christendom; his real knight—as distinguished from the burlesque Sir Thopas—is not a buffoon, like Cervantes': he merits Chaucer's and the reader's respect, and he gets it; but one does not get the impression that his son or anyone else will re-enact the pattern of his life. The quests and the Crusades are equally archaic for Chaucer, as they are for Spenser, and the twenty-two-line portrait of the twenty-year-old squire is as characteristic a picture of the Renaissance gentleman as one could wish. He has almost all the notes

of the conduct-books: the external comeliness and harmonious-
ness; the strength; the martial ability (for its own sake: Urbanite
English campaigning in Urbanite Flanders was not major war-
fare); the skill in horsemanship, in musical composition, in
dancing, drawing, poetry, and writing in general; the propriety
in dress; the courtesy; and if his loving is more active than
Castiglione's Bembo would approve, Bembo makes allowance
for excesses in youth.

If the picture scarcely seems to fit Chaucer himself, many
elements in his own life and work are characteristic in other
respects of the Renaissance poet and man of letters: royal
patronage; youthful military service; travels and diplomatic
service; dedication to learning; reverence for classical authors;
concern with contemporary learning in other vernaculars as
well as in Latin; poetic experimentation; concern with, and
practice of, translation; a distinctly urban and urbane approach
to life; theological depth and awareness, combined with a clear-
eyed perception of institutional inadequacies and distortions; the
prizing of proportion and balance in art, of courtesy, sincerity,
and gentilesse in man. He was even hailed neoclassically by his
contemporary, Eustache Deschamps, "as a Socrates in philosophy, a Seneca in morality, an Aulus Gellius in practical affairs,
and an Ovid in poetry." Professor Charles W. Dunn, after
quoting these words, once wrote that "such effusive praise [is]
rarely accorded to a writer within his own lifetime"; but the
words are so characteristic of the complimentary mode of the
Renaissance that one must rather think that few Renaissance
men and women of any note could have escaped in their life-
times hearing something like them about themselves.[1] And it
is Chaucer, not Wyatt or Howard, who first translated into
English verse a sonnet of Petrarch.

The kinship and respect that almost all English poets of the sixteenth century felt for Chaucer reflect their recognition that he had been the chief beginner of modern English letters, and thus a significant initiator of the new age in England. Indeed, the general respect for Chaucer may have been a continuing cause of sixteenth-century English inconsistency in judging or defining their present age with regard to the past. When the religious debates and bitterness had led most literate Englishmen to repudiate the national learning and literature of the centuries just before the first Tudor's accession, Chaucer remained a massive qualification or exception, and for many he must have occasioned serious doubts as to whether the present intellectual ambiance was that much more alive and healthy than—or different from—the one in which Chaucer had flourished and won wide recognition. One may, at least, find a certain urbane irony in Sir Philip Sidney's famous statement: "I knowe not whether to mervaile more, either that hee in that mistie time could see so clearly, or that wee in this cleare age, goe so stumblingly after him."

Similarly, many Englishmen of Sidney's time who were accustomed to think of pre-Tudor, pre-Reformation times as misty, dark, and culturally much inferior to their own, must have paused when they recalled the musical innovations of John Dunstable and the reputed role of that early fifteenth-century Englishman in the development of what we now call Renaissance music (see Professor Lowinsky's paper below).

In any event, the confusion and inconsistency about chronological and cultural self-definition occasioned in sixteenth-century England by the approximate coincidence of the elements mentioned above—the Tudor dynasty, western exploration and discoveries, printing, the renewed interest in Greek studies, and religious reform—make contemporary English evidence on the true nature of the English Renaissance uncertain and often paradoxical. Moreover, the confusion and inconsistency seem to have endured in much of the writing in English about the Renaissance, to the serious disadvantage, necessarily, of Renaissance scholarship in the English language. Two continuing circumstances, indeed, have reinforced the difficulty since the sixteenth century. One is that Shakespeare, however he may himself have seen the fifteenth century in relation to his own time, turned it forever into history with a genius and a finality that no literary giant has applied to the Tudor or any subsequent era. The other is that for most English-speaking men and women, the Renaissance has never been nearly so interesting or seemed nearly so important to the subsequent history of the world as either the Reformation or the beginnings of the extraordinary historical movement which was to spread the English language and English literature and institutions to every continent in the world. One small side effect has been that for most historians of English literature, few things have seemed more clearly certain than that Chaucer is (almost by definition) a medieval poet, or at most a premature dawn of the Renaissance in England.

Outside England, of course, the chronological convergence was not operative in people's self-definition within history—not, at least, with regard to those circumstances of human life and thought which can be described properly as the Renaissance. Certainly Tudors instead of Plantagenets in London could make little difference to the self-awareness of men and women at the Sorbonne or in Urbino. In Italy—and it is still there that one naturally turns first for primary evidence on most aspects of the Renaissance—printing and Atlantic adventures and religious revisionism of the sort that culminated in the Protestant Reformation were scarcely substantive elements in the Renaissance, a complex of changes which predated all of them by at least several decades.

One turns, then, to contemporary Italian evidence (and to pertinent Continental sources in general) with more assurance of finding a clearer sense of what was truly and importantly characteristic of the Renaissance, a less paradoxical awareness of what was directly relevant to the Renaissance as such, and what was simply contemporaneous with it or followed it closely in time.

We must seek such direct evidence if we are to correct the "partialities," whether conscious or unconscious, of post-Renaissance scholarship; and in interpreting English testimony it is wise to let Continental Renaissance sources provide a corrective for whatever is insular or provincial in the England of the Tudors, at least. This the present collection of papers can help us to do. Moreover, the direct testimony of Renaissance men and women changes complexion and texture according to the habitual preoccupations and the range (both intellectual and imaginative) of the witnesses: philosophers do not often see their age or their own place within it as musicians and poets do; mathematicians, theologians, sculptors, and painters are likely to have different perspectives and different landmarks or *points de repère* within those perspectives. It is, then, eminently useful to have the testimony of many kinds of witnesses: this, too, is part of the intention of the present volume.

One does well, also, to recall constantly that Gascoigne's suggested prayer for historiographers has two parts: the man who wishes to see the Renaissance must constantly test his vision for the blindness caused by partialities; and in listening to the direct or indirect testimony of those who lived during that age, he must not trust too much "in every tattling tongue." The man of one book may be "proverbially formidable to all conversational figurantes," but he is *formidabilis* in more than one sense: it can be as risky to take all the eggs out of one basket as to put them all in one, and too much reliance on a single source or even a single kind of evidence has often been a concealed trap to those seeking to understand a past age. To adapt a quip used by Professor Bush in his paper in this volume, Goldwater and Galbraith cannot easily be shown to agree in their interpretation of what is most important about our own time, and the scholar of the future will have to balance their testimony with that also of witnesses as diverse as Yevtushenko, Charles de Gaulle, Picasso, Bertrand Russell, Orff, John XXIII, Sartre, and James Baldwin. Too much trust in any one of them—not that "tattling tongues" is an apt collective description—will give the scholar of 2450 an incomplete view of the way in which "men in the 1960's" saw themselves and their times, if in some instances perhaps a better view than we shall have deserved.

By at once correcting past partialities with scholarly breadth and precision, and using primary Renaissance sources with sensitivity and discrimination, the papers that follow contribute individually and conjunctively to a better understanding of the Renaissance as it appeared to many of the people who made it and experienced it.

1. Charles W. Dunn, *A Chaucer Reader* (New York, 1952), p. xi; and see below, pp. 37 and 111.

THE RENAISSANCE IMAGE OF MAN AND THE WORLD

authors use
of footnotes
pictures
graphs

Every source + document
used - credit was given

PHILOSOPHY AND HUMANISM
IN RENAISSANCE PERSPECTIVE

By

Paul Oskar Kristeller

IN A SENSE we cannot help seeing the past from the point of view of the present since we shall never get away from the present or from our place in it, and certainly historians have a right to impose their own modern categories on the past which they are trying to understand. However, certain aspects of the past may be overlooked or misunderstood because familiar things were called by different names (for example, literary criticism was once called rhetoric, and physical science was called natural philosophy) or because familiar words were once used with a meaning that greatly differs from the present one (for example, such terms as "humanist" or "liberal arts"). Hence, we may hope to gain a better understanding of the past if we try to recapture its categories, as far as that is possible, and to become conscious and critical of our own categories even where we cannot avoid using them.

My topic is rather broad for treatment in a short space; in any event, the state of present scholarship (i.e., my own and many other people's ignorance, to use a phrase of Petrarch's) and the difficulties and complexities of the topic itself preclude the full and adequate treatment that it clearly deserves. I shall limit myself to a few general points which are inevitably based on recent scholarly discussions as well as on my own reading in the period. I must apologize, then, if here I repeat to a certain extent what has been said before by others and by me: I cannot create new basic facts for this paper, and it has not been my intention to recast radically my own previous conclusions.

I should like to begin with the place which philosophy and humanism occupied within the framework of Renaissance learning and civilization. It is a question in which I became interested when I tried to understand the links that connected Renaissance humanism and Renaissance scholasticism, especially in Italy, with the academic, professional, and literary traditions of the later Middle Ages.[1] Such a question is always difficult to answer for philosophy. For philosophy is often understood in such a broad and elusive way that it appears to be involved in any kind of reflective thinking that may be included in theology, or the sciences, or literature, or even in the actual conduct of life. If we limit ourselves to philosophy as a distinct intellectual and, as it were, professional enterprise, its definition and its relation to other disciplines are subject to great variety, depending on the historical period, on the specific school and tradition, and even on the orientation of individual thinkers. Also, "humanism" seems to be exposed to similar difficulties as the term becomes the tool of popular discussion and the butt of scholarly controversies. The Renaissance did not use the term "humanism," but it coined the terms "humanist" and "humanities," and it is comparatively easy to make out from the documents what the period understood by the humanities, namely, a cycle of studies that included grammar, rhetoric, poetry, history, and moral philosophy, and involved the study of the ancient Greek and Latin authors. The best known, and probably the earliest, document is the library canon composed by Nicholas V as a young man; and the same text also makes it clear that theology, jurisprudence, medicine, mathematics, and the philosophical disciplines of logic, physics, and metaphysics were not included among the humanities. The testimony of this document has been confirmed by many others; and to my knowledge, it has not yet been refuted by contrary evidence. As soon as such counterevidence is forthcoming, I shall be glad to revise my interpretation of Renaissance humanism. In the meantime, I venture to be unimpressed when distinguished colleagues assure me that they do not like this interpretation or that some different views held by themselves or their predecessors are still true in a higher sense. Yet, if we take the Renaissance description of the humanities seriously, as I am inclined to do, we shall also understand why the work of the humanists spans the territory of several disciplines that have been distinct in modern times: humanists were classical scholars and historians, poets and prose writers, literary critics and political theorists, and they were philosophers, especially moral philosophers. The contribution each humanist made to any of these fields varies greatly in quality and quantity; yet it is important to realize that for a Renaissance humanist they formed a connected, if not unified, whole which he was inclined to consider as his proper domain. On the other hand, these disciplines have become quite distinct and even separate in modern times, and this has affected the scholarly study of their past history. Thus the historians of literature and literary criticism, of historiography and political thought, of educational theory and practice, of classical scholarship and philosophy, have all been concerned with Renaissance humanism, but each of these groups of historians has tended to interpret humanism more or less exclusively in terms of the contribution it made to his particular subject, and largely ignored the other aspects of humanism and, above all, the broader conception underlying its peculiar range and combination of intellectual interests. To bring under a common denominator what we have learned about the humanists as writers, as classical scholars and copyists, as historians and philosophers, seems almost hopeless at the present hour, and to this we may add certain other aspects of their work that have found but scanty favor among modern historians, such as their theory and practice of oratory and of letter-writing. Yet this is obviously what we should aim for if we want to understand Renaissance humanism and its place and role during its own time. To this, we must add an objective study of the impact humanism had upon those subjects and traditions that were not a part of the humanities as then understood. In asserting and defending the claims of their own studies, the humanists attacked their rivals in other fields, the theologians, the logicians and natural philosophers, the physicians, the jurists. This criticism, though often unfair, was surely stimulating, and gradually the humanists contributed to the transformation of all other fields: they extended and improved the study of relevant classical sources, introduced different standards of historical criticism, new ideals of literary presentation, and an emphasis on new problems. Consequently, the humanists deserve a place also in the history of theology and jurisprudence, of the sciences, of the philosophical disciplines other than ethics, and even of the arts and of music. And of course, there were several individual humanists who combined their humanist training and interest with professional competence in some of those other subjects. There were humanists who were also artists like Alberti, theologians like Erasmus and Melanchthon, jurists like Alciato or Cujas, physicians like Vesalius, or metaphysicians like Vives.

Yet if we want to understand the full meaning of philosophy in the Renaissance, we must not limit ourselves to the work of the humanists as philosophers and especially as moralists. The Renaissance inherited from the thirteenth and fourteenth centuries a different concept of philosophy that was rooted in the scholastic traditions of the universities. Since the thirteenth century at least, philosophy has been taught as a subject of its own, distinct from the liberal arts and from theology, and largely on the basis of the writings of Aristotle and of his commentators. The philosophical disciplines as taught included logic and natural philosophy, which were the most important subjects, as well as metaphysics and ethics. Natural philosophy contained several disciplines that have subsequently become sciences separate from philosophy and from each other, such as physics, biology, and psychology, and hence its development has been largely studied by historians of science, whereas the historians of philosophy have concentrated on the other disciplines that are still considered as belonging to philosophy: logic, metaphysics, and ethics (historians of aesthetics must be satisfied with chance remarks, and otherwise turn to the treatises on poetics and rhetoric, on painting, architecture, and music for their sources). Metaphysics had obvious connections with theology, and was sometimes taught by theologians; but in spite of overlapping subject matter, it was a philosophical discipline distinct from theology, if not in conflict with it. To put it crudely, Aristotle's *Metaphysics* had a somewhat different content from the Scriptures or Peter Lombard's *Sentences*. The course on ethics included also political and economic theory and the theory of passions as treated in Aristotle's *Rhetoric,* as we can see from many documents. It was in the field of ethics that the Aristotelian philosophers really competed with the humanists, and it is no coincidence that moral philosophy occurs twice in the canon of Nicholas V, once among the disciplines of Aristotelian philosophy, and once among the humanities. Whether the course on ethics at a Renaissance university was taught by an Aristotelian philosopher or a humanist depended on personalities and local arrangements. It did make a difference, of course, as to method and emphasis, terminology, and even the translation used, and this is an interesting subject that, in my opinion, has not yet been sufficiently explored. Yet it should be remembered, whereas it is often forgotten, that the bulk of the teaching and study of the philosophical disciplines other than ethics, and of the sciences then considered as parts of philosophy, was carried on through the sixteenth century by scholastic or Aristotelian philosophers, who include such distinguished figures as Pomponazzi or Zabarella, and who may have been influenced in various ways by humanism, but who represent a different tradition. Until recently, these Aristotelians have fared rather badly with most historians of philosophy, and with many they still do. Even the historians of science have paid scanty attention to them. After they have discovered the scientific contributions of the fourteenth-century Aristotelians at Oxford and Paris, most of them still blame the humanists for not having continued this tradition (which was not their tradition anyway) and fail to see that the tradition was actually continued by the Italian scholastics of the fifteenth and sixteen centuries—again a wide field for further study that has been barely touched.[2]

To sum up, the conception and place of philosophy in the Renaissance are characterized by two competing intellectual traditions, humanism and Aristotelian scholasticism, which partly overlap and quarrel, but largely coexist in a kind of division of labor. If we want to use contemporary analogies, we might say that there was a philosophy oriented toward the sciences, and another that was oriented toward the humanities, and actually the scholastics were philosophers and scientists, and the humanists were philosophers and scholars. If I seem to have given the impression in some of my past statements that I consider the Aristotelians as the "true" philosophers of the Renaissance, or the humanists as mere rhetoricians who were not truly philosophers in the professional sense of the word, I wish to retract, because my views have been exaggerated by others, and because I do not wish to endorse the present tendency among English and American philosophers to emphasize the sciences and to ignore the humanities. In terms of Renaissance studies, the scholastics and their role have been unduly neglected, and this may have been my reason for stressing their importance. Yet actually, both sides in the struggle have their merits and their shortcomings, and a philosopher should be in a position to view them in a detached fashion. To use ancient terms, if the scholastics stressed *scientia* and the humanists *eloquentia*, our aim should be to combine both of them with *sapientia*. Hence I feel in sympathy with the Platonist Pico della Mirandola when he defended the medieval scholastics against the humanist Ermolao Barbaro; for this was not a rejection of humanism by a traditionalist, but an effort to achieve a synthesis of what was valuable in both traditions on the part of one who had absorbed them both.[3] I shall not attempt to discuss in this paper the relationships of Renaissance philosophy and humanism to the theology and religious thought of the period. These relationships are complicated, and they varied from case to case; and to do them justice, it would be necessary to dedicate an entire paper to this subject alone. For our purpose it may be sufficient to say that the Renaissance treated the various philosophical, humanistic, and scientific disciplines as distinct from, though not necessarily opposed to, theology and, in doing so, merely continued and expanded a tradition well established in the Middle Ages at least since the thirteenth century.

After having discussed the place which humanism and philosophy seem to have occupied on the intellectual globe of their time, I should like to turn next to the historical role which the thinkers of the Renaissance assigned to themselves, which they aimed at fulfilling, and which they sometimes believed they had actually fulfilled. As you well know, the humanists looked with respect and admiration upon classical antiquity and more or less bitterly attacked the Middle Ages; they tried in many ways to imitate the former and to abandon the traditions of the latter. In countless statements most of which have been collected for us by Ferguson and Weisinger and other scholars, the humanists spoke of the ancient eloquence and poetry, letters and arts, learning and wisdom that were being reborn in their own time after a long period of decay and that were being brought back to light after the darkness of many centuries.[4] It is this very notion which underlies the customary division of Western history into antiquity, the Middle Ages, and the modern period, which produced the popular notion of the Dark Ages, and which led modern historians to give the name "Renaissance" to the period that marked the beginning of the modern age. The objective value of this whole conception has been challenged in recent decades by many medievalists and other historians; and we should be ready to admit, on the basis of our much increased knowledge, that the later medieval centuries were hardly so dark as to require a completely new light and that the claims of the humanists, though perhaps justified to some extent and in certain areas, are quite exaggerated if taken in their broadest meaning and at their face value. Moreover, a comparison of the numerous statements in which the claim is expressed has shown that they vary greatly in emphasis, in the areas of culture for which a rebirth is asserted or demanded, and in the precise time and persons to which this rebirth is attributed. And it is easy to show that the claim often degenerated into an empty slogan when every renowned philosopher or physician was called another Aristotle or another Hippocrates, and when a rebirth was occasionally claimed even for Averroism or for Ockhamism. Finally, it has been shown that the notion of a revival of poetry not only goes back in Italy to the early fourteenth century (and this disposes, for good, of Burdach's attempt to derive the secular slogan via Cola di Rienzo from medieval religious conceptions) but it can even be found in a few ancient and medieval authors. St. Ambrose is credited by St. Augustine with a revival of eloquence, Lanfranc of Pavia and Canterbury is praised by his biographer for having restored Latinity to its ancient state of knowledge; and ever since Carolingian times, the political idea of the Roman Empire had been linked with the notion that ancient Rome had been renewed. But when all this is said, the fact remains that Renaissance literature, and especially humanist literature, is full of this notion which was applied by Vasari to the visual arts, by Machiavelli to politics, by the religious humanists to Christianity, by Ficino to Platonic philosophy, and, at least by implication, by the humanist Aristotelians even to the philosophy of Aristotle. Hence, even if we are most skeptical (as I am not) about the achievements of Renaissance humanism and about its claim of having brought about a Renaissance of learning, we must admit that the so-called Renaissance was at least that period in Western history when people were convinced that they were witnessing or bringing about a renaissance of letters and of learning; and in case we lack a better definition, we might as well define the Renaissance as the period in which there was the most frequent talk about the Renaissance of learning.

Yet again, as in the case of the ideal of the humanities, a careful survey of Renaissance thought will show that the idea of a rebirth was not universally held by the philosophers or even by all humanists of the period, but that there were other important conceptions competing with it and partly opposed to it. The writings of the humanists are full of pessimistic remarks about the state of letters and learning in their own time, and many of them were convinced that the achievements of the ancients could never be equaled.[5] Machiavelli insists that human nature is the same at all times;[6] and although he ostensibly uses this as an argument for our ability to imitate the ancients, the notion has quite different implications, and the two are not necessarily connected. The view that human nature is always the same is also implied by Montaigne,[7] and it has for him the same pessimistic implications as for Machiavelli, yet he does not link it with the idea of rebirth at all. There is constant change, to be sure, but it is not a change for the better; and if the present age seems to have overcome some of the errors and limitations of its predecessor, this merely means that it must expect to have its own errors corrected by a future age.[8] The scholastic Aristotelians certainly felt that they were continuing without a break the work of their medieval predecessors. And although the Platonic philosophers spoke at times of the revival of ancient Platonic wisdom,[9] they were much more concerned with the steady continuity of human wisdom through the course of Western history and with the universal diffusion of truth among all peoples and at all times. Marsilio Ficino believed that there was a continuous tradition of philosophy that began with the renowned writings attributed to Hermes Trismegistus, Zoroaster, Orpheus, and Pythagoras (writings which we know to be apocryphal products of late antiquity) and stretched through Socrates and Plato to the Platonic schools of later antiquity, and through the Byzantine, Arabic, and medieval Platonists down to Cusanus and to himself.[10] Pico della Mirandola added Aristotle and his Greek, Arabic, and Latin interpreters as well as the Jewish cabalists to the list, and gave expression to the view that all of them, at least in some of their assertions, had a share in universal truth.[11] These notions were widely held by thinkers of the sixteenth century, and it was in the Platonic tradition that a theologian in sympathy with it coined the term "philosophia perennis,"[12] a term that has since been appropriated by other traditions but that seems to fit Platonism as well as any other school of philosophy. The Platonists' conception of the history of philosophy and of their own place in it seems to be as significant as the humanist idea of revival or rebirth, and it enjoyed a great vogue. It supplied the background for many later ideas on tolerance, on natural religion, and on natural law, and should be considered as one of the sources of later deism.

Finally, Renaissance thought contains many germs of the modern idea of progress, which is fundamentally opposed to that of revival. Whereas most humanists were convinced that their own age was inferior to that of the ancients or at best could match some of their achievements, the question whether the moderns could surpass the ancients was raised already in the fifteenth century, and sometimes was answered in the affirmative.[13] As the sixteenth century went on, the voices in favor of modern superiority multiplied.[14] Aside from contemporary achievements in the arts and sciences, the invention of gunpowder and of the printing press and the discovery of America were most frequently cited as instances of modern progress. In this way, the ground was laid for the battle of the ancients and moderns; and whereas this controversy became most vocal in the seventeenth century, it has been recently shown that it had some of its roots in the sixteenth and even in the fifteenth centuries.[15] In the field of philosophy, as in that of the sciences, there was a strong feeling, often rebellious, that a thinker should assert his originality and his independence of the ancient authorities, such as Aristotle and Galen. New ideas, new systems, had to be formulated, and it is especially clear with the philosophers of nature from Paracelsus to Bruno that they claimed and believed to be new and original in their ideas. Telesio, though full of respect for the Aristotelian tradition in which he had been brought up, tried to replace it with his work on nature according to its own principles;[16] and Patrizi, although a professed Platonist, called his main work a "new philosophy" of the universe.[17] Modern scholarship has again tended to show that these thinkers were not as new and original as they thought they were, but the historical fact remains that they aimed at being original (although they may not have achieved this aim completely), just as their predecessors aimed at being faithful interpreters of Aristotle or of Plato (although they may actually have been less faithful and more original than they realized). Francis Bacon, who challenged Aristotle by writing his *Novum Organum,* was an heir of this Renaissance tradition. And in Galileo there is already a strong feeling that there was a lot of knowledge and a lot of truth that had not yet been known and that remained for the present and the future to be discovered and demonstrated.[18]

Having discussed the views held by Renaissance humanists and philosophers of their role in history, I should like now to approach our problem from a third and last angle and discuss the tasks they assigned to philosophy in human life and the notion they had of the philosopher and of his mission. If we begin again with the humanists, it is quite clear from their writings that they thought of themselves primarily as moral philosophers and that they considered ethics as the most important, the only essential, part of philosophy.[19] This attitude can be clearly traced from Petrarch to Montaigne, and it has significant implications. Only those problems that are of direct human concern are worth talking and writing about, and the problems of logic, of physics, and of metaphysics are unimportant since they have no bearing on us, on our conduct, and on our happiness. It is this attitude that has led some scholars to compare the humanists with the existentialists of our own day. On the other hand, the humanists maintained that the study of rhetoric and poetry, of history and of the ancient authors, which they advocated and cultivated, had a formative influence on the moral character and thought of the students and thus was of great human concern. This explains the humanist preoccupation with education and with the school which they actually subjected to a reform whose effects have been felt for many centuries almost until our own time.[20] It is this human significance of their studies that led the humanists to call them "humanities," a term from which the name for their own profession and movement derived, as we have seen. This central concern for moral thought and for man also explains why the dignity of man was a favorite topic with many humanists, a theme which was developed also by philosophers like Ficino, Pico, and Pomponazzi, whom we are reluctant to call humanists, although they were no doubt affected to a varying degree by the humanist learning of their time. On the other hand, it is well known that the praise of man's dignity also had its strong opponents, that is, not only the Protestant reformers, but also Montaigne who in many other ways may be considered a representative of humanism.

If we want to understand more concretely the moral and philosophical ideals of the humanists, we cannot help paying attention to a question that has been much discussed both by the humanists themselves and by their modern interpreters, namely, the relative merits of the active and the contemplative life. Through a number of brilliant studies, we have become acquainted with a republican or civic humanism which flourished especially in Florence during the first half of the fifteenth century and found its most eloquent representatives in Salutati, Bruni, Alberti, and Palmieri.[21] These writers seem to advocate in their treatises the active life of the businessman, citizen, and statesman rather than the contemplative life of the mere scholar or philosopher. Other scholars have extended the picture into the sixteenth century and have concluded that the main trend of Renaissance thought was to abandon the medieval monastic ideal of contemplation and to put in its place the modern ideal of action, that is, an action enlightened by thought and experience.[22] There are, I agree, texts which seem to confirm this theory; certainly Renaissance thought, following Cicero rather than the Greek philosophers, recognized the values inherent in the active life to a greater extent than had the thought of the preceding period, and no doubt this fact has its historical significance. Yet it is not true that the Renais-

sance, or even Renaissance humanism, speaks with a single voice
for the superiority of the active over the contemplative life.
The Platonist philosophers and most of the Aristotelians clearly
favor the life of contemplation and consider action merely as
an imperfect image of thought. Pomponazzi does connect the
goal of human life with the practical rather than with the
speculative intellect, and this emphasis is doubly significant
because it differs from that of Aristotle. Yet he does not main-
tain that the activity of the practical intellect is higher than
that of the speculative intellect, but merely that it may be
attained by a much larger number of persons.[23] Among the
humanists themselves, we find many who clearly favor the life
of contemplation, not only Landino who was influenced by
Ficino's Platonism, but also Petrarch and many others. Even
most of the humanists who have been cited as the main witnesses
of the active ideal seem to express at times a different view.
Salutati wrote an entire treatise, which has been recently
published for the first time, to prove the value and even the
superiority of the monastic life.[24] Alberti in his treatise on the
family does speak with favor of the busy life of the merchant,
to be sure, but in his other moral writings he insists that only
the quiet life of philosophical reason can give us real satisfaction
and enable us to withstand the blows of chance that are otherwise beyond our control—views that are reminiscent of ancient
Stoicism and that are encountered in the works of many other
humanists.[25] Even Leonardo Bruni does not consistently place
the active life above that of contemplation, but rather sees the
ideal in a combination of the two[26] or states that the contemplative life is more divine, and the active life more useful,[27]
and thus comes pretty close to the position of Aristotle himself.[28]
I cannot help feeling that these apparent contradictions or

hesitations may be due to the occasion on which a given statement was written and to the persons for which it was intended.
A humanist rhetorician cannot help praising the active life when
writing of and for a businessman or a statesman or even a
prince (for the life of action is not limited to republics), and
even Ficino would do the same in a similar context, as some
of his letters clearly show.[29] On the other hand, the life of
contemplation would get its due share when the person addressed
or involved is a monk, as in Salutati's case, or a philosopher,
scholar, or scientist, as in most other instances. As a matter of
fact, for the Renaissance thinker the life of contemplation is
not primarily the monastic life. If it is true that the Renaissance
reduced the importance of the monastic ideal, it opposed to it
not only the ideal of the active businessman or statesman but
also that of the philosopher and scholar who was not necessarily
a monk or cleric. Speaking more broadly, I do not think that
the respective claims of the contemplative and the active life
have been settled once and for all by the Renaissance in favor
of the active life. These are competing ideals which are rooted
in human nature, and the contemplative life has had its advocates among the leading philosophers of all times, in the
Renaissance no less than in the subsequent centuries or in our
own time, and it is likely to have them also in future times.[30]
Yet coming back to the Renaissance discussion, we must ask
in each instance whether a writer is advocating the ideal of
the active life only for others to whom he addresses himself or
also for himself. It is quite clear that most humanists conceive
of themselves primarily as scholars, whatever advice they give
to others, and that Pomponazzi is conscious of being a philosopher rather than a member of the ordinary crowd for which
he may formulate a generous ideal but to which he feels

superior through his knowledge and his ability of reasoning.[31]
An unqualified approval of the active life is rather rare in the
Renaissance, and we would expect to find it only in those
writers who would identify themselves wholeheartedly as states-
men rather than as scholars or philosophers. This is not the case
of Leonardo Bruni who certainly was a statesman, but whose
death was lamented, as his beautiful epitaph in S. Croce in
Florence says, by history and eloquence, and by the Greek
and Latin Muses (if not by philosophy).[32]

If we turn from the humanists to the other, more professional
philosophers of the period, we move still further away from the
ideal of the active life. The Platonist Ficino believes in the
superiority of the contemplative life, as we have seen; but, even
more, contemplation, in the sense of metaphysical speculation
and of the direct vision of God and of the intelligible world of
ideas, represents for him, as for the ancient Platonists, the true
goal and content of human existence.[33] The true philosopher is
for him the person who attains this knowledge and experience
and conveys its substance to others through his teaching and
writing. The Platonic philosopher is also called a theologian,
not because Ficino happened to be a priest or had studied
dogmatic theology based on Scripture and authority, but because
the Platonic philosopher attained through reason and contemplation and through his philosophical authorities a truth about
God and the intelligible world that was in basic agreement with
dogmatic theology, but derived from independent sources.[34] It
was this wisdom acquired through contemplation that enabled
the Platonic philosopher to withstand the power of chance, to
choose the right course of action according to the circumstances,
and to overcome the limitations of the external sensuous life
by which the ordinary people are enslaved. The philosopher

will laugh and cry with Democritus and Heraclitus at their folly and misery.[35] He knows that our ordinary thoughts are but shadowy dreams, and thus he alone is awake among so many sleepers.[36] Yet unlike Plotinus and his other ancient models, Ficino is not convinced that the philosopher can permanently escape the plight of ordinary human existence. Man's quest and thirst for the infinite makes him forever restless during his earthly life. The philosopher attains the vision for a short while, but he cannot retain it. He is superior to other human beings because he knows our goal, and he is aware of the limitations and deficiencies of ordinary earthly existence, but in a way he suffers more than others who do not know what they lack. For this reason, Saturn is the star of the intellectuals, and their temperament is melancholy. This suffering will be overcome only in a future life when the vision of God will be attained forever and without limitations.[37]

If Ficino's notion of the waking and restless philosopher reflects a vision that can be attained though not permanently fulfilled during our present life and still resembles in some of its undertones St. Augustine's restless search for God, Pomponazzi's much more sober thought arrives in an unexpected way at a quite similar picture of the philosopher. He does not believe, with the Platonists, in the possibility of attaining during the present life a direct and, as it were, natural knowledge of God and the intelligible world. For him, as an Aristotelian philosopher, we have no other sources of knowledge but sense perception and the faculty of reasoning. His method does not consist in the approximative description of a valid knowledge previously and directly attained, as for the Platonists, but in the ever-renewed effort to follow a rational discourse and argument from given premises, wherever it may lead him. Hence the strained and complex and even contradictory manner of his writing. In a strange and isolated passage, Pomponazzi suddenly expresses his troubled feelings and compares himself with Prometheus, the prototype of the philosopher who is eaten up by his worries and thoughts while trying to know the secrets of God, persecuted by the inquisitors, and held up to ridicule by the ordinary crowd.[38] Clearly Pomponazzi was no less aware or proud of the philosopher's task than Ficino had been, no less convinced that he was called upon to overcome the illusions of the ordinary crowd, and that he had to pay a price in suffering for his greater knowledge.

Finally we may compare with this what another philosopher who really was neither a Platonist nor an Aristotelian, though closer to being the former, had to say about the life and task of the philosopher. Giordano Bruno associates the philosophical life with the heroic love of which he treats at great length in one of his dialogues, the *Eroici Furori*. Like Pomponazzi, he uses a mythological figure to illustrate the struggle and suffering inherent in the life of reason. Commenting on a sonnet of Tansillo about Actaeon who was turned by Diana into a stag and torn by his own hounds, Bruno explains that this myth refers to the heroic love and to the heroic intellect. For Actaeon symbolizes the intellect as it is searching for divine wisdom and tries to grasp divine beauty. He is thus transformed into his very object, and pursued and torn apart by his own thoughts.[39]

I do not wish to impose upon these occasional remarks and symbols a greater and wider importance than they have, but I find them striking and characteristic. They seem to show, as some of the other ideas we mentioned did, that for many thinkers of the Renaissance, philosophy had its own task and

(47)

mission distinct from the common moral ideals of ordinary human life, and that this philosophical ideal was conceived as valid for all times and not limited to the demands of a passing historical situation. I hope to have shown that in Renaissance thought the contemplative life did not lack its defenders, though the values of the active life may have been more widely and more explicitly recognized than in previous centuries. More generally, I intended to show that some of the views on philosophy and its task that are commonly associated with humanism and with Renaissance thought were not held by all philosophers of the period, and not even by all humanists. I do not deny that these views were held by some humanists and that they are intrinsically and historically important, but I feel that we must interpret these views with greater subtlety and with many more qualifications than has frequently been done and must pay greater attention to the divergent opinions expressed by the humanists themselves and by their contemporaries. Yet I do not claim to have presented an adequate or definitive analysis of this complex problem, and I am convinced that a more careful and more comprehensive reading of the relevant sources may eventually lead to different and perhaps quite unexpected conclusions.

If I may draw a further lesson from the ideas which I have been trying to survey, I should like to emphasize that philosophy and scholarship have a permanent task to fulfil at any time, beyond the immediate actual tasks which they may be called upon to perform within a given situation. When we are confronted with opinions that may contain an element of truth (how else could they be seriously held by anybody?) but that are clearly exaggerated in the form in which they have been expressed, it is tempting and perhaps even inevitable to counter one exaggeration with an opposite one. Yet in the long run it seems more satisfactory to aim, not at a mere compromise between given opinions, but at a synthesis in which the legitimate core of each different opinion is somehow included. Yet in formulating this ideal, I am already voting for the contemplative and against the active life, I must admit, and committing myself to the view, probably not shared by all of my colleagues, that this is the choice befitting a philosopher and a scholar.

1. For the following discussion, see my article, "Humanism and Scholasticism in the Italian Renaissance," *Byzantion*, XVII (1944–45), 346–74, reprinted in my *Studies in Renaissance Thought and Letters* (Rome, 1956), pp. 553–83, and again in my *Renaissance Thought* (New York, 1961), pp. 92–119, 153–66.

2. Much information is scattered in P. Duhem, *Etudes sur Léonard de Vinci* (3 vols.; Paris, 1906–13). A pioneer monograph is Marshall Clagett, *Giovanni Marliani and Late Medieval Physics* (New York, 1941). Especially misleading and defective in this respect is the widely quoted book by A. C. Crombie, *From Augustine to Galileo* (London, 1952).

3. Q. Breen, "Giovanni Pico della Mirandola on the Conflict of Philosophy and Rhetoric," *Journal of the History of Ideas*, XIII (1952), 384–526.

4. Wallace K. Ferguson, *The Renaissance in Historical Thought* (Boston, 1948), especially chap. i. Herbert Weisinger, "Renaissance Accounts of the Revival of Learning," *Studies in Philology*, XLV (1948), 105–18, and several earlier papers. See also Erwin Panofsky, *Renaissance and Renascences in Western Art* (Stockholm, 1960), chap. i. G. Ladner, "Vegetation Symbolism and the Concept of Renaissance," *De artibus opuscula, XL: Essays in Honor of Erwin Panofsky* (New York, 1961), 303–322.

5. Charles Trinkaus, *Adversity's Noblemen: The Renaissance Humanists on Happiness* (New York, 1940).

6. *Discorsi* i. prologue; chaps. 11, 39; iii. chap 43: " . . . tutte le cose del mondo in ogni tempo hanno il proprio riscontro con gli antichi tempi. Il che nasce perchè essendo quelle operate dagli uomini, che hanno ed ebbono sempre le medesime passioni, conviene di necessità che le sortischino il medesimo effetto."

7. *Essais*, Bk. II, No. 12, ed. J. Plattard, Vol. II, Pt. 1 (Paris, 1947), p. 183: " . . . il est entravé et engagé, il est assubjecty de pareille obligation que les autres créatures de son ordre. . . . "

8. *Ibid.*, pp. 352–53.

9. Marsilius Ficinus, *Opera* (Basel, 1576, reprinted Turin, 1959), p. 944.

10. P. O. Kristeller, *Il pensiero filosofico di Marsilio Ficino* (Florence, 1953), pp. 16–20 (*The Philosophy of Marsilio Ficino* [New York, 1943], pp. 25–29). Cf. R. Klibansky, *The Continuity of the Platonic Tradition during the Middle Ages* (London, 1939 and 1950), pp. 42–47.

11. Pico, *Oratio* (*De hominis dignitate . . .*, ed. E. Garin [Florence, 1942]), pp. 101–65; *Conclusiones* (*Opera* [Basel, 1572]), pp. 63–113. Cf. A. Dulles, *Princeps Concordiae* (Cambridge, Mass., 1941); E. Garin, *Giovanni Pico della Mirandola* (Florence, 1937); E. Anagnine, *G. Pico della Mirandola* (Bari, 1937).

12. Augustinus Steuchus, *De perenni philosophia libri X* (Lyons, 1540).

13. G. Margiotta, *Le origini italiane de la Querelle des anciens et des modernes* (Rome, 1953). H. Baron, "The *Querelle* of the Ancients and the Moderns as a Problem for Renaissance Scholarship," *Journal of the History of Ideas*, XX (1959), 3–22. A. Buck, "Aus der Vorgeschichte der *Querelle des anciens et des modernes* in Mittelalter und Renaissance," *Bibliothèque d'Humanisme et Renaissance*, XX (1958), 527–41.

14. J. B. Bury, *The Idea of Progress* (London, 1920), chap. i. H. Weisinger, "Ideas of History during the Renaissance," *Journal of the History of Ideas*, VI (1945), 415–33.

15. See note 13, above.

16. B. Telesius, *De rerum natura iuxta propria principia* (Rome, 1565).

17. F. Patricius, *Nova de universis philosophia* (Ferrara, 1591).

18. Letter to the Grand Duchess Cristina: "E chi vuol por termini alli umani ingegni? chi vorrà asserire già essersi veduto e saputo tutto quello che è al mondo di sensibile e di scibile?—Non si dovrà . . . precluder la strada al libero filosofare circa le cose del mondo e della natura, quasi che elleno sien di già state con certezza ritrovate e palesate tutte."—Galileo Galilei, *Le opere*, V (Florence, 1895), 320–21.

19. Cf. P. O. Kristeller, "The Moral Thought of Renaissance Humanism," in *Chapters in Western Civilization* (3rd ed.; New York, 1961), I, 289–335.

20. W. H. Woodward, *Vittorino da Feltre and Other Humanist Educators* (Cambridge, 1905); *Studies in Education during the Age of the Renaissance* (Cambridge, 1906). E. Garin, *L'educazione umanistica in Italia* (Bari, 1949); *L'educazione in Europa* (*1400–1600*) (Bari, 1957); *Il pensiero pedagogico dello umanesimo* (Florence, 1958).

21. H. Baron, *The Crisis of the Early Italian Renaissance* (2 vols.; Princeton, N.J., 1955); *Humanistic and Political Literature in Florence and Venice at the Beginning of the Quattrocento* (Cambridge, Mass., 1955).

22. Eugene F. Rice, Jr., *The Renaissance Idea of Wisdom* (Cambridge, Mass., 1958).

23. P. Pomponatius, *De immortalitate animae* (1516), chap. 14 (translated by W. H. Hay in *The Renaissance Philosophy of Man*, ed. E. Cassirer et al. [Chicago, 1948], pp. 350–77, esp. 353–57).

24. C. Salutatus, *De seculo et religione*, ed. B. L. Ullman (Florence, 1957).

25. P. H. Michel, *Un ideal humain au XV*ᵉ *siècle: La pensée de L. B. Alberti* (Paris, 1930).

26. Leonardo Bruni Aretino, *Humanistisch—Philosophische Schriften*, ed. H. Baron (Leipzig and Berlin, 1928), pp. 72–73: "Cum itaque duae sint ut ita dixerim vitae, una negotiosa et civilis in agendo reposita, in qua iustitia temperantia fortitudo ceteraeque morales virtutes dominantur, altera otiosa contemplationi vacans, in qua sapientia et mens et scientia ceteraeque intellectivae virtutes locum habent, video philosophos illos qui optimi fuerunt in utraque istarum permulta tradidisse tum convenientia fidei tum utilissima ad disciplinam et cognitionem nostram, quae et recipienda sunt et in usum nostrum vertenda."

27. *Ibid.*, p. 39: "Utraque sane vita laudes commendationesque proprias habet. Contemplativa quidem divinior plane atque rarior, activa vero in communi utilitate praestantior."

28. *Nicomachean Ethics* x. 7–8.

29. *Opera*, pp. 744–45, 778–79.

30. I am indebted to Professor Howard Rienstra for a number of passages from G. B. della Porta and Federico Cesi, which show that by the end of the Renaissance the terms "contemplation" and "speculation" became associated with scientific inquiry.

31. *Op. cit.*, pp. 364–65. See also note 38, below.

32. "Historia luget, eloquentia muta est, ferturque Musas tum Graecas tum Latinas lacrimas tenere non potuisse."

33. Cf. *The Philosophy of Marsilio Ficino*, chap. xii.

34. *Ibid.*, pp. 24–29, 316–23.

35. *Opera*, pp. 636–38.

36. *Ibid.*, pp. 316–17. Cf. p. 628: "Theologi vigilant, caeteri somniant."

37. *The Philosophy of Marsilio Ficino*, chap. xi.

38. P. Pomponatius, *Libri quinque de fato, de libero arbitrio et de prae-destinatione*, ed. R. Lemay (Zurich, 1957), Bk. iii, chap. vii, p. 262: "Prometheus vere est philosophus qui dum vult scire Dei archana perpetuis curis et cogitationibus roditur, non sitit, non famescit, non dormit, non comedit, non expuit, ab omnibus irridetur et tanquam stultus et sacrilegus habetur, ab inquisitoribus prosequitur, fit spectaculum vulgi. Haec igitur sunt lucra philosophorum, haec est eorum merces."

39. Giordano Bruno, *Des fureurs héroïques*, ed. P.–H. Michel (Paris, 1954), Pt. 1, dialogue iv, pp. 205–9.

THE RENAISSANCE:
THE LITERARY CLIMATE

By

Douglas Bush

BEFORE we ask how Renaissance writers conceived of themselves
and their world and literature, we may for a moment glance at
modern theories. Around 1900 there was one fairly simple,
almost unquestioned concept of the Renaissance, or the Italian
Renaissance. That concept was the composite product of a
number of notable historians and thinkers, of whom Burckhardt
had been the chief. It was also a natural product of the liberalism
of the eighteenth and nineteenth centuries, and it stressed
whatever elements in the Renaissance seemed to herald that
movement: man's discovery of the world and himself; the over-
throw of authority by secular, naturalistic individualism; the
conquest of asceticism by aestheticism; and so on. This is still
the popular formula and, in less simple terms, it retains among
scholars a degree, a widely varying degree, of validity. There
were some early challenges. Greatly enlarged knowledge of
the Middle Ages rejected the notion of an awakening after a
long sleep; and, from a similar point of view, the picture of

neopagan Italy was toned down to admit the existence of order, orthodoxy, pietism. During this past generation, widened and deepened learning and discriminating insights have so greatly illuminated and complicated "the Renaissance" that specialists walk warily through a maze of qualifications, and amateurs like me are stopped in their tracks. Facing the complexities and contradictions of theories and evidence, one can only envy the feverish patient whose doctor said, "You may read either Galbraith or Goldwater but not both."

In much modern discussion of the Renaissance the importance of the classical revival seems to have greatly shrunk, but a student of literature can hardly acquiesce in that change of focus. Moreover, the literature of half a dozen countries and a couple of centuries cannot be neatly packaged and labeled, and a short sketch may well emphasize the classics, the great common ground on which almost all writers stood. If to any moderns some formative ideals and principles appear obsolete and tedious, for leading minds of the Renaissance they were dynamic realities; and conceivably our own age would be better off if we could or would recover some of them. Any doubts concerning the fertilizing power of the classics—along with many other stimulating forces, to be sure—may be quieted by the thought of a few great names, Machiavelli and Ariosto, Rabelais and Montaigne, Cervantes and Shakespeare. If, as we go on, I draw mainly upon English examples, it is because they are most familiar to most of us and, in a large perspective, sufficiently typical of the Renaissance as a whole.

Even if we knew no history, abstract logic would tell us that a classical—that is, an educational—revival would follow the barbarian invasions and develop with growing momentum. Its quickened flowering in Italy from the fourteenth to the sixteenth century was the natural result of French influence, of increasing resources and knowledge, multiplying apostles and disciples, the contagion of enthusiasm and self-confidence, the opportunities and rewards open to humanistic scholars, and the generally favorable climate of the affluent city-states. The similar if slower process which had been at work in remoter parts of the old Roman world, such as Britain, was increasingly stimulated by Italian influence. Not to cite the many witnesses to early classical ardor in Italy, we may remember the excitement of Erasmus when, having left Paris for a first visit to England, he encountered John Colet, Thomas More, and their group; or the contrast drawn by Rabelais' Gargantua between the illiberal time of his youth and the fever for learning that now possessed old and young. Earlier scholars and writers did not know that they were living in the Middle Ages; their successors were very much aware that they were men of the Renaissance—and, with their far greater knowledge, they had a far more historical view of antiquity. We might recall, incidentally, that such early and learned interpreters as Bacon and Milton saw the European classical revival as a by-product of the Reformation; and in sixteenth-century England the phrase "the new learning" meant Protestantism, not the classics.

Greek and Roman literature and thought had comprehended wide diversities and conflicts, and these were perpetuated, heightened, and complicated during the Renaissance; but in a brief and broad survey we may think, as at times Renaissance men could, of a unified Graeco-Roman culture—or rather, of a unified Graeco-Roman-Christian culture. For large-minded humanists the assimilation and re-expression of that culture meant not only continuity with a great past and the hope of a great future, it meant universal solidarity in the present. All over Europe, boys and young men—prospective lawyers, states-men, clerics, scientists—were studying the same body of material in much the same way. From the early fifteenth century down at least to Milton's tract, books on education were written—unlike most modern books on the subject—by the most eminent scholars of Europe as well as by humble pedagogues; and in all these, family likenesses far outweighed national or religious or individual differences. A common culture by no means extinguished such differences, but it could transcend them. Thus the best of all courtesy books, Castiglione's *Courtier,* embodied the most urbane ideal of the cultivated gentleman and lady and of life conceived and practiced as a fine art; whereas Sir Thomas Elyot's *Governor,* in its title and its earnest, unsophisticated text, embodied practical concern with the education of the ruling class. The one book is as Italian as the other is English, yet both derive from the Platonic and Ciceronian conceptions of the philosopher-king and the orator as representative of the ideal type of virtue, wisdom, and civic responsibility.

The classics, in nourishing the rational man, nourished the critical spirit in scholars like Lorenzo Valla and in historians, philosophers, and scientists. Yet that critical spirit rather strengthened than sapped the idealism and universal solidarity I speak of. In a general way, it was felt that the clear-eyed ancients had seen and distilled the truth about all kinds of human experience. Erasmus' first book, his often-enlarged and very popular collection of classical adages, with comments, presented an attractive picture of a civilization signally endowed with sanity, wisdom, and pithy utterance; and in many books Erasmus carried on the critical spirit of Valla along with the practical piety of Colet. His very critical if not very pious contemporary, Machiavelli, appears in a rarely winning light in the much-quoted passage from a letter written when he was out of office and occupied on his small estate: returning home at nightfall and exchanging muddy clothes for courtly attire, he would sit down in his study to discourse with the great men of ancient Rome and inquire into their motives, "and these men in their humanity reply to me, and for the space of four hours I feel no weariness, remember no trouble, no longer fear poverty, no longer dread death; my whole being is absorbed in them." Toward the end of the century, even so skeptical and critical a moralist as Montaigne gladly acknowledged his large and constant debts to Seneca and Plutarch—although these sages might not have acknowledged some of their disciple's doctrines.

Without unduly idealizing the Renaissance or ignoring its many crosscurrents, one cannot contemplate such basic solidarity without thinking of the continual fissions and the esoteric advances in modern knowledge, which have caused so much concern over the failure of communication among and even within our many diverse disciplines. The Renaissance ideal of the many-sided amateur had numerous actual exemplars from Leonardo and Castiglione to Sir Philip Sidney and Bacon; the modern ideal, or the inevitable product of the modern world, seems to be the single-minded expert. A partly parallel contrast appears in the field of imaginative literature. In modern discussion no topic is more familiar than the problem of the artist's isolation from society. The Renaissance, to be sure, had its highbrow, middlebrow, and lowbrow divisions; many humanists and writers were more or less dependent on patrons and scorned the profane vulgar; and the gentleman-author did not breathe the air of the market place. Yet, in obvious ways and for obvious reasons, there was far more cultural homogeneity, and the writer—Shakespeare, for instance—was much more in harmony with the relatively uniform outlook of his audience than modern writers are likely to be with their heterogeneous public.

It is quite impossible to exaggerate the veneration that Renaissance scholars and most writers felt for the Romans and Greeks as superior races of beings, the supreme exponents of literary art, the supreme oracles of rational wisdom, the creators of the golden age of civilization. Deeply conscious, at least for some time, of their own inferiority, they strove to emulate the ancients in the hope of attaining a comparable degree of sweetness and light. As modern scholars have shown, the humanists were fully, not to say overweeningly, aware of their role and achievement. From, say, Leonardo Bruni and Flavio Biondo in the earlier fifteenth century up to Louis Le Roy in the later sixteenth, they saw the revival of letters and learning as a distinct era in the long course of cultural and intellectual history; Le Roy, the professor of Greek, is a witness of special interest because his name is identified with the modernist gospel of progress. The earlier and even later humanists knew that to look forward they must first look backward—a long way back, beyond what they saw as a desert of monkery, scholastic logic, and bad Latin. Most literary revolutions start from a leap over immediate predecessors to older, richer, fresher sources of inspiration, and no revolution was more zealous or more conservative than the Renaissance return to the fountains, both secular and religious. As a main or initial clue we may take the motive of imitation, a motive which could often be mistaken but could also be profoundly right. From the naïve, stubborn, and touching Ciceronianism of the old man that Petrarch tells about, we might jump up to the English Renaissance. In his *Arte of Rhetorique* (1553; 1560), Thomas Wilson expressed typical humanistic piety:

> Now, before we use either to write, or speake eloquently, wee must dedicate our myndes wholy, to followe the most wise and learned men, and seeke to fashion as wel their speache and gesturing, as their witte or endyting. The which when we earnestly mynd to doe, we can not but in time appere somewhat like them.

Nearly a century later came Milton's *Of Education,* a program based, like the many earlier tracts of European humanists, on ancient models (though now with a large addition of science); and Milton, having brought his students to the point of reading the great tragedies and orations, said, in a spirit akin to Wilson's, "which if they were not only read, but some of them got by memory, and solemnly pronounced with right accent and grace, as might be taught, would endue them even with the spirit and vigor of Demosthenes or Cicero, Euripides or Sophocles." Milton's own career epitomizes, on a level of high civic and religious fervor, the full span of humanistic ideals, the combination of discipleship to the classics and public service. Yet, for him as for Ben Jonson and other writers of power, the ancients were "Guides, not Commanders"; and the output of the greatest classical artist of the modern world is the grand example of a poet working within a tradition and, with inspired originality, re-creating every classical genre he touched, from ode to tragedy.

The first kind of imitation—with which Milton began—was naturally the writing of Latin verse and prose. This was no novelty. What the humanists added to medieval practice was a much more informed, more strict, and more conscious elegance. The impulse was powerful enough to endure in education up through the nineteenth century. In the Renaissance centuries it produced an enormous mass of neo-Latin verse and many famous names, such as the Italian Petrarch, Poliziano, Pontano, Mantuan, Sannazaro, Castiglione, Vida, and Alciati; the Dutch Secundus and Grotius; the Polish Casimir Sarbiewski; the Scottish George Buchanan; and the English Sir Thomas More, John Owen, Crashaw, and Milton. I might say that, in making a large commentary on Milton's Latin poems, I have read a ton of neo-Latin verse, with respect if not with passion. Most of it has long vanished below even the scholarly horizon, but in its own age it was for generations more important than the emerging literature in the vernaculars; Petrarch cherished his epic *Africa* (and his Latin treatises) more than the Italian poetry which gave him his lasting fame. Even Milton could debate with himself about whether to write his epic in Latin or, by writing in English, to forfeit his desire for a European audience; and we may remember that in speaking of the question Milton cited the advice given to Ariosto by Cardinal Bembo, the *arbiter elegantiarum* of early sixteenth-century Italy. We cannot doubt (*pace* C. S. Lewis) that the writing of neo-Latin verse contributed much to the growth and maintenance of a universal European culture. Its influence upon the form and texture of vernacular poetry has not been fully studied, and would be difficult to disengage from classical influence, but one large external fact was the abandonment of most medieval genres for the classical epigram, satire, epistle, pastoral, ode, epic, comedy, and tragedy.

Before Milton posed his question, Bacon had said that these modern languages would play the bankrupts with books, and he put his own writings into Latin—which reminds us that the progress of science would have been greatly impeded if scientists had not used the international language. It would have been at least equally calamitous if Erasmus had written in Dutch; as it was, he had more influence than any other writer of his age, more, probably, than all but two or three men in modern history. A few works of neo-Latin prose, unlike neo-Latin poetry, survive in popular as well as scholarly repute, notably *The Praise of Folly* and *Utopia;* both books are conspicuous examples of the original and forceful adaptation of classical forms—and classical irony—to contemporary life and problems. In the seventeenth century, Robert Burton and Sir Thomas Browne planned to write their scientific works in Latin but shifted, happily, to English. We may remember that university students read, wrote, and spoke Latin as a second native language; in such a climate it was difficult for anyone to have a provincial outlook.

Even a glance at neo-Latin prose should not pass over one phenomenon. The slavish imitation of Cicero's style could, mainly in Italy and France, lead to the absurdities that Erasmus satirized in his *Ciceronianus;* Erasmus himself revered Cicero the moralist but abhorred devotion to the letter rather than the spirit of classicism. Yet the general cultivation of Ciceronian Latin, or, in broader terms, the study of rhetoric, must not be judged by its frivolous or pedantic excesses. Latin was both a practical and professional necessity and the key to ancient and much modern knowledge, thought, and literature, and writers needed a disciplined, civilized standard; moreover, rhetoric involved logic and close study of all the processes of thought and composition. Nearly a century after Erasmus' satire, Bacon censured Ciceronianism as one of the three chief "vanities" which had hindered the advancement of true learning; he was, as a sort of Jacobean John Dewey, condemning traditional literary education. When Bacon says, "Here therefore is the first distemper of learning, when men study words and not matter," his hostile echo of a phrase of the Tudor humanist, Roger Ascham, has large reverberations. Ascham had said: "Ye know not, what hurt ye do to learning, that care not for wordes, but for matter. . . . " But the context of that saying goes far beyond good Latin as an end in itself. Ascham is speaking of style as the index and instrument of moral and social order or disorder. We might move up to a later classical humanist, Matthew Arnold, and recall Lionel Trilling's remark that whenever Arnold talks about style, he is really talking about society. Or there is that resolute nonconformist, the late George Orwell, who wrote specifically of language and style as the symptom of cultural and political health or disease. At the present moment the widespread and flagrant abuse of English reflects the state of our world.

It may be stretching the letter, though not the broad idea, of "imitation" to include here the vast and valuable work of the army of translators in all countries who turned the corpus of Greek literature into Latin, Latin and Greek into the modern languages, and, finally, modern literature from one language to another. Most of the greatest translations in English were those made in the sixteenth and earlier seventeenth centuries: those of the Bible; North's Plutarch; Florio's Montaigne; the scholarly Philemon Holland's Livy and other historical works; Shelton's *Don Quixote*; Urquhart's Rabelais; and, in verse, Chapman's heroic versions of the Homer whom he worshiped as the supreme poet and teacher. A multitude of other translations, from Golding's Ovid to Sylvester's rendering of Du Bartas' epic of creation, were more or less important in their age. Translation was not, as it was to be in later centuries, a gentleman's elegant pastime; it had serious and solid motives. Translators labored with patriotic zeal to make the sources of knowledge

and wisdom available to their unlearned countrymen and to
enrich their own literature and language. A typical exemplar is
Sir Thomas Hoby, the translator of Castiglione's *Courtier,* who
in 1561 affirmed that in translation "Englishmen are much
inferiour to most of all other Nations," and who urged Greek
and Latin scholars to make translations, "And so shall we per-
chaunce in time become as famous in England, as the learned
men of other nations have bene and presently are"; he found
his own task difficult, but "I whetted my stile and setled my
selfe to take in hand the other three bookes." One modern
tribute paid to Hoby's work is that, if it had not been circu-
lating for forty years, Benedick and Beatrice could not have
been born. Arthur Golding, carrying on a medieval and allegorical conception of Ovid—a conception which by no means
precluded aesthetic enjoyment—showed with full illustration
that the *Metamorphoses* contained invaluable moral lessons for
both sexes and all ages. The expressed motives of the biblical
translators, from Tyndale onward, were, of course, the most
earnest and exalted. Chapman was hardly less earnest in his
ethical view of Homer, a view which led to continual coloring
of his text; and I must quote from his preface to the *Odyssey*
a sentence I am fond of quoting. Chapman thus contrasts
Achilles with his ideal hero, Odysseus:

> In one, Predominant Perturbation; in the other, over-ruling
> Wisedome; in one, the Bodies fervour and fashion of outward
> Fortitude, to all possible height of Heroicall Action; in the
> other, the Minds inward, constant, and unconquerd Empire;
> unbroken, unalterd, with any most insolent, and tyrannous
> infliction.

Translators, in England and elsewhere, were not always precisely faithful, and they might work more or less from inter-

mediaries, as North did from Amyot, but, thanks to their period, their motives, and their gifts, they wrote with racy vitality and flavor, not in "translators' English."

We arrive at the heterogeneous mass of literature in the modern languages and, first of all, at imitation of the classics in these. To say a word about prose style, in our own age we assume that prose just gets written; there are no schools of theory and practice—unless the title be given to those who preach that there is no standard of good English, that whatever anyone uses is right. But sixteenth-century Europe inherited a concern with rhetoric which had been active since the Greeks, and England had its full share. Some Tudor prose, in the *Book of Common Prayer* or the Bible or Sir Thomas North, is both homely and magnificent, but much of it is immature and undisciplined. One effort to tidy it up was Euphuism, an English version of a European phenomenon. Ciceronian English had barely reached a first maturity in Hooker when Continental anti-Ciceronianism came in and brought about a repetition of what had occurred in ancient Rome. The Ciceronian period, which was adapted for the rotund utterance of public and accepted verities, gave way to Senecan and Tacitean prose of either a loose or a clipped and pointed kind. The new mode, like contemporary metaphysical poetry, lent itself to the tentative exploration of private, everyday experience, and, as we might expect, it was first employed by the early essayists. Bacon is a link between this movement and the later effort of scientists to achieve a bare, exactly denotative prose suitable for exposition.

In poetry, imitation could be disastrously wrongheaded. Of the many poets who dreamed of writing the great modern epic, one was the prince of lyrists, Ronsard, who complacently warned the readers of his epic that if they did not have the ancients in mind, it would be a dead weight in their hands; but there was no "if" about it. In his short poems Ronsard's classicism—which included the Hellenism of his time and group—was an active inspiration and discipline. In general, since our interest is in the positive and vital elements of Renaissance doctrine and practice, we may slight the manifestations of a shallow and barren classicism, such as snob appeal, neopaganism, dilettantism, pedantic formalism; corresponding diseases attend all movements in all ages—witness nowadays the aberrations of some myth-and-symbol criticism or some abstract painting. It was the fault of individuals as well as the creed if for three or four centuries Europe was littered with epics and dramas frozen from birth in *rigor mortis*. We may remember George Brandes' happy phrase about Voltaire, that the man who respected little in heaven or earth respected the uniform caesura.

In formal ways poets in the vernaculars carried on to some degree the same program as the neo-Latinists (and a number worked in both media). In addition to taking over the classical genres, sporadic or systematic attempts were made in Italy, France, and England to introduce classical meters; this idea of order was, in the infancy of modern poetry and in the more moderate theories, less mad than to our hindsight it may now appear. As for the dramatic rules codified from Aristotle and Horace, they, as everyone knows, did not win much authority in England, where the strength of medieval and popular tradition and individual genius brought about the great efflorescence of unclassical drama. The chief or only English neoclassicist was Ben Jonson, and Jonson was no Malherbe. In English nondramatic literature the most representative poet was Spenser, who, though he naturalized some classical genres in England, can hardly be called a classicist. It is a commonplace that his poetry is a confluence of classical, Italian, French, and native traditions, but these are only elements in a pot more pregnant than Donne's, though modern critics—as distinguished from scholars—prefer ignoring him to understanding him. Here, however, we cannot do more than recall a few familiar points about his artistic and moral attitudes and his background.

We often think of the pastoral as the most artificial of all poetic kinds, yet it had enough vitality to last for two thousand years, mainly because at the start Theocritus and Virgil had exploited not only its idyllic attractions but its value as a vehicle for any personal or public subject a poet wished to treat. While *The Shepherd's Calendar*, as poetry, has only minor claims upon us, it was a manifesto of a new mode, and it is a microcosmic specimen of Spenser's eclectic approach to his art. The title came from a popular almanac; the poet enthroned Chaucer as his tutelary genius; in the tradition of Bembo and the Pléiade, he revived much archaic diction; his very diverse metrical experiments included both rough popular meters and sophisticated elegance; and some poems were topical and satirical. At the same time, Spenser used the forms and themes and materials of classical and Renaissance eclogues (with a novel framework); and "E.K.," as editor of *The Shepherd's Calendar*, though often mistaken, was at pains to stress the new poet's awareness of decorum and to link motifs, allusions, and rhetorical devices with ancient, medieval, and modern conventions.) Also, E.K. recognized the pastoral as the appropriate first flight for a poet—a reminder that Virgil's career was or was becoming an established model.

The Faerie Queene is not so readily pigeonholed, and Gabriel Harvey's phrase about an early sample of it is the first comment on its eclecticism. In that, Spenser went far beyond his modern predecessors. The Renaissance, though happy to follow Aristotle in most things, departed from him in setting up the epic rather than tragedy as the supreme poetic genre, and, as we have observed, many poets dreamed of being the modern Homer or Virgil. But the great heroic poems of the sixteenth century, *Orlando Furioso, Jerusalem Delivered,* the *Lusiad,* and *The Faerie Queene,* are all more or less unclassical and more or less alive. The Italian debate over the *Orlando*—was it or was it not an epic?—reached the judicious conclusion that if Aristotle had known it, he would have approved. Ariosto, by the way, might be called the Ovid of the Renaissance; along with many specific debts, he had his own large stock of Ovidian inventiveness, buoyancy, and irony, and, we must add, the predominant lack of seriousness of a pure Ovidian artist. Tasso made his poem a unified if still highly romantic tale. If Spenser went beyond Tasso and even Ariosto in variety of matter and tone, he did so too in weighted subtlety of texture and in moral and religious depth and complexity. That depth and complexity can only be assumed or asserted here, but, as we all know, during the past forty years a number of scholarly critics have been expounding a new Spenser, freed from the blight of nineteenth-century misconceptions.

Spenser's prefatory letter to Ralegh, with its soberly ethical interpretation of the great heroic poets, Homer, Virgil, Ariosto, and Tasso, is one small and familiar expression of the didactic theory of literature which the Renaissance inherited and developed. Certainly a great deal of Renaissance writing, like a great deal of ancient writing, was far from being morally instructive. None the less, the ancient theory of literature, from Plato and Aristotle to Horace and Plutarch, was strongly ethical or openly didactic; even the rowdy Aristophanes declared it the function of poetry to make good citizens. Much Renaissance criticism, more Horatian and practical than Aristotelian, proclaimed the expressly didactic view that poetry should delight and move and thereby teach, and that view was shared by many imaginative writers. Even Ariosto had his allegory or *exemplum* of the temperate man, and Tasso contrived an allegory *ex post facto*. Spenser's declaration of his purpose everyone knows; likewise his use of both allegory and ethical types. Spingarn long ago began his standard book with the statement that "the first problem of Renaissance criticism was the justification of imaginative literature." The didactic justification followed two main lines. On the one hand, there was the tradition of allegorical truth contained in fiction, a doctrine which had been active before Plato and which was widely expounded and applied in the Middle Ages, notably by Boccaccio (who did not apply it to the *Decameron*). Until the recovery of Aristotle's *Poetics,* with its aesthetic principle of ideal imitation, the imaginative reality which has a universal truth beyond particulars, allegory was the only theoretical basis available for the defense of literature. Nor was it quickly displaced by Aristotle. It was appealed to by almost all the Elizabethan defenders of poetry, even by the easygoing Sir John Harington in the preface to his version of Ariosto. The notable exception was Sir Philip Sidney, who passed by allegory and invoked Aristotelian doctrine. At the same time, Sidney was fully in accord with his fellows, and with Renaissance criticism at large, in his repeated emphasis on the moral value of examples of virtue and vice—a concrete emphasis which, like most of the essay, is more Platonic than Aristotelian. To us, for whom contemporary fiction and drama rarely provide any but bad examples, the Renaissance creed may appear distressingly naïve; yet it did not cripple, and it surely helped to nourish, much of our greatest writing. The rebellious, naturalistic Renaissance had an immeasurable belief in the efficacy of moral *exempla* and *sententiae*.

Reference to allegory and ideal examples invites a word about one conspicuous medium for both, classical mythology. This vein had been freely tapped in medieval literature for narrative, allusion, and allegorical meaning; and in the Renaissance these uses were carried to a plenitude and richness never approached again until the romantic age. On the purely literary plane, the handling of myth was the great illustration of *ut pictura poesis*, and its quality was paralleled on acres of canvas. Italianate warmth and lusciousness of description, which left the highly pictorial Ovid far behind, spread over all Europe. If such sensuousness—which embraced much more than mythology was one kind of Renaissance idealism that might be called neopagan, much of it was not. The flesh and the senses offered temptations to be overcome; Circe had many sisters and cousins. But even in the briefest allusions, mythological figures and images had a universal value. In Shakespeare and almost all poets, the gods and goddesses stand for ideal beauty and grace or greatness; they can be, as it were, pagan counterparts of the angels, types of superhuman power and passion. And simple idealism may be undercut by irony. Helen of Troy, whose face launched a thousand poets, was the supreme incarnation of mortal beauty and youth and love, the supreme object of the natural man's desire—and yet, for the impassioned Faustus, she was an illusion of the devil and could not make him immortal with a kiss.

Behind such glowing visions, such symbols of the super-human, were Ovid and other poets old and new and also the mythographers whose dictionaries of myth included traditional

(69)

allegorical interpretations. Boccaccio's handbook was still in use but mainly superseded by later and more learned ones like that of Natalis Comes; even Bacon wrote a book in which he allegorized myths, mainly in scientific and civil or political terms. Renaissance poets, such as Spenser, Chapman, and Jonson, used these works as modern poets have used *The Golden Bough*. It is not easy to draw a line between naïve allegorizing and sophisticated symbolism, and Renaissance literature has an abundance of both. Finally, there was the effort to reconcile pagan fiction with moral and Christian truth; the one could be seen as a distorted version of the other. Hence classical myth could be freely employed in Christian settings; Christ, the good shepherd, could be Pan, the god of shepherds. The young Milton illustrates the general flexibility: in his fifth Latin elegy, on the coming of spring, his senses revel innocently in mythological and sexual images of nature, while in the *Nativity* the birth of Christ puts the pagan divinities to rout.

We come, finally, to the ethical, religious, and metaphysical beliefs and ideas that were a common heritage. It seems to me logically clear and historically sound to take the medieval tradition of Christian humanism as the main road and to see on one diverging road the increasing number of non-Christian humanists, the indifferent or skeptical, and, on a diverging road on the other side, the increasing and much larger number of non-humanistic Christians, Catholic and Protestant. Much Renaissance thought and literature cannot be understood if we slight the continuing impulse to reconcile nature and grace, pagan reason and Christian faith. On the philosophic plane, no one labored more zealously than Ficino, whom Professor Kristeller has expounded, to fuse Platonic philosophy with Christianity. On a more practical level was Erasmus, the Christian humanist par excellence, whose double aim was imitation of classical wisdom and of Christ, who found prime allies in Plato and Cicero, and who distilled the two great saving traditions in that inspired phrase, "Sancte Socrates, ora pro nobis." Many teachers, scholars, and writers, from Vittorino da Feltre to Milton, carried on the ideal of "virtue and good letters." Modern writers have often spoken of *studia humanitatis* as if the name implied opposition to theology; sometimes it did, but in the orthodox view these studies were complementary, not antagonistic. As Cicero, the oracle and model of Renaissance humanism, had said, *sapientia* is the knowledge of things human and divine. Or, as Aquinas had said, grace does not abolish nature but perfects it. The ancient and basic conflict between Augustine and Pelagius was revived between Luther and Erasmus; Erasmus, with his ideal of rational religion and of human capacities, was charged with Pelagian exaltation of man at the expense of God and grace. Yet the rational Erasmus, in the midst of his survey of human folly and corruption, could suddenly startle his readers with a paradoxical glance at the supremely irrational folly of Christ and true Christians; such ironic idealism rises above even the Socratic, and it is hardly fanciful to leap over a century from Erasmus to Cervantes.

Granted a large variety of religious and irreligious, philosophical and unphilosophical minds and writings, we are looking at the orthodox. Every student of English literature at least is familiar with that all-embracing principle of order, the great chain of being; the same hierarchical principle ordered the levels of society and the mental faculties of man. With the Christian doctrine of obedience to God was merged the ethical psychology of Plato and Aristotle, rational control of the irrational appetites and passions. What God is in the macrocosmic universe, God-given reason is in the human microcosm. Moreover, this is not merely reason in our sense: it is the Christianized Stoic faculty of "right reason," *rectu ratio*. Plato had provided the two necessary conditions for this concept, the existence of ethical-metaphysical absolutes and man's ability to apprehend them. Thus, although right reason can be misled by human weakness and although the truths necessary for salvation are known only through revelation, the collective right reason of mankind has established the laws of nature. Hence Richard Hooker can make what may seem a very bold affirmation for a divine: "The general and perpetual voice of men is as the sentence of God himself. For that which all men have at all times learned, Nature herself must needs have taught; and God being the author of Nature, her voice is but his instrument." These words explain the philosophic basis of Christian humanism, the rational Christian's acceptance of pagan thought as, with all its deficiencies, a partial anticipation and natural ally of Christian faith.

For many writers these and related doctrines might have little or no actuality, but all writers were more or less conditioned by living in a world theoretically or vehemently committed to a Catholic or Protestant creed. And very few writers, whatever their practice, would have denied Christianity itself. Some took a fideistic line and, like Montaigne, kept their religious belief or profession and their reason in separate compartments. For example, Montaigne quoted a phrase from Seneca which Samuel Daniel thus versified—

> And that unlesse above himselfe he can
> Erect himselfe, how poore a thing is man—

But the idea that Daniel approved, Montaigne rejected as exhibiting human presumption in a situation that only grace could repair. With the Catholic Montaigne would be Luther, Calvin, and the darkly Calvinistic Fulke Greville, Daniel's patron and friend, while on Daniel's side would be, say, such Christian Stoics as Chapman and Jonson. This is one small example of ideological complexities.

We might well ask ourselves where the greatest Renaissance writer stood, although a paragraph or two cannot get very far into a question on which many books have been written. We may be hesitant about trying to pin down the personal beliefs and attitudes of a poet who spoke through dramatic characters, yet modern interpreters seem to be pretty well agreed that Shakespeare shared the Protestant orthodoxy of his fellow citizens, however far his imaginative insight might carry him beyond popular fundamentalism. Through the history plays runs the conception of Providence opposing human wickedness, a conception found in the sources and in most contemporary English historians, such as Sir Walter Ralegh. Hamlet is sustained by the same belief, and sees himself as heaven's scourge and minister; and Malcolm, about to lead an avenging army against Macbeth, declares that "the powers above/ Put on their instruments." Apart from the innumerable specific allusions to matters of belief, which often seem to have more than dramatic authenticity, few readers would deny a Christian tone in plays as different as *King Lear* and *The Tempest*. To say this is not to go along with the more extreme arguments for "the Christian Shakespeare" that recent times have brought forth.

A poet like Chapman, who urgently expounds an ethical creed, can not only borrow ideas and illustrations but versify many and long segments from his humanistic sources, ancient and modern. While we expect no such thing in the undoctrinaire Shakespeare, still, as we all know, he contains a good deal of Renaissance ideology. Whether or not he assimilated Montaigne, his background is not what T. S. Eliot unhappily described as "the mixed and muddled scepticism of the Renaissance." The most famous example of Shakespearian philosophizing is, of course, the speech of Ulysses in the third scene of *Troilus and Cressida,* the *locus classicus* for the principle of order and degree and the great chain of being. As Harry Levin has pointed out, the speaker, not Shakespeare, but a "wily strategist" in a crisis, treats the ideas of order "as a set of norms which are currently violated. Far from reaffirming the *status quo,* he reveals the abyss that so closely underlay the surfaces of Elizabethan awareness. . . . Thence Ulysses continues, envisioning the cosmos as an unappeased struggle for power. . . . " These cautionary words are well said; but at least the norms were there. Many have thought that in writing this speech Shakespeare remembered the opening pages of Elyot's *Governor* and Hooker; at any rate he was writing in the tradition they represent. Similar ideas come up again, in the Archbishop of Canterbury's speech in the second scene of *Henry V* and the gardener's scene in *Richard II* (III.iv).

The middle station of man in the great chain of being had large implications. As Pico della Mirandola had said in his famous discourse, the Creator gave to man at his birth the capacity to sink to the animal or rise to the divine. A main source of the strength of Renaissance literature is the active sense of the perpetual contrast or conflict between the bestial and the angelic impulses in human nature, between what man is and what he would or could be. It is on that theme that Burton begins the *Anatomy of Melancholy.* It can be more or less comic, as in Shakespearian comedy or Rabelais or Cervantes, or it can be tragic, with or without religious motives. When the naturalistic Montaigne expresses his general satisfaction with himself as he is, he does so in the hierarchical terms: he has neither an angel's conscience nor a horse's conscience but a man's conscience. The deeply troubled Donne uses similar terms to describe himself:

> I am a little world made cunningly
> Of Elements, and an Angelike spright;
> But blacke sinne hath betraid to endlesse night
> My worlds both parts, and (oh) both parts must die.

There is no need of illustrating the constant operation of the double vision in Shakespeare.

This rapid sketch, a partial summary of what everyone knows, has perhaps recalled enough signposts to justify the claims made for the conscious respect for tradition, the conscious quest of order, the predominant sanity of the Renaissance in its literary expression. To say this is not to say that the literature was tame and timid. Many names have reminded us that in this age the theory and practice of imitation led into the richest and boldest creativity (and that had its theory, too). It might be argued that of all ages in history the Renaissance was the most healthy; one sign of health is that it produced most of the great English tragedies and almost all the great English meditations on death. In life and in literature the age contained, in a kind of dynamic equilibrium, active traditionalism and active originality, elegant refinement and brutal violence, invincible idealism and destructive skepticism, the fact of disorder and the ideal of order. One grand reason for the health and sanity, the heroic dimensions, of Renaissance writing is that this was the last age in which the fullest drama of the natural man was enacted against the religious background of good and evil, heaven and hell. And if not all men had a religious sense of good and evil, few could avoid looking up to some beings higher than themselves and worthy of imitation, whether the Greek and Roman authors and statesmen or the heroes of epic and romance or the gods of mythology or Christ and the angels and saints. On whatever level such beliefs and attitudes existed, Renaissance men were more likely than those of other ages to recognize their kinship with both the godlike and the bestial.

THE IMAGE OF MAN IN RENAISSANCE ART: FROM DONATELLO TO MICHELANGELO

By

H. W. Janson

SINCE the Renaissance is a vast and complex area, I shall confine my remarks to a particular section of it: the Florentine Early and High Renaissance. Or, if we are to express these limits in political terms, the span of slightly more than a century that began about 1400 with Leonardo Bruni's *Laudatio Florentinae Urbis* and the city's successful defiance of Giangaleazzo Visconti and ended in 1512 with the re-entry of the Medici into Florence and the crushing of the republican spirit in the city. I propose, in other words, to include in my discussion the Michelangelo of the "David" but not the Michelangelo of the Medici tombs. Such a limitation is not wholly arbitrary; it will permit me to cover only one chapter of my subject—the new image of man in Renaissance art—but perhaps the decisive one: the creation of the new image in the first half of the fifteenth century and that phase of Michelangelo's art which still reflects his awareness of this basic achievement. After 1512, it seems to me, such an awareness plays a less and less significant part in Michelangelo's work.

I must acknowledge a further limitation: I have tried to confine myself to works of art about which we have sufficient data to let us see them, to some extent at least, as the Renaissance itself saw them. For the period under consideration, this is quite a severe limitation. Viewed in isolation, statues and paintings are mute witnesses, and direct verbal testimony about specific works of art is rare indeed until the mid-sixteenth century, the time of Vasari. Nor can we take Vasari's words at face value when they concern works of art created a century or more before his day. The Renaissance view of art and artists underwent decisive changes during the second quarter of the Cinquecento,[1] so that we must use extreme caution in accepting judgments or interpretations of Early Renaissance art by Vasari and his contemporaries. If we want to learn how the men of the period 1400–1512 viewed the artistic achievements of their day, we shall have to rely very largely on indirect testimony— evidence gathered from the unself-conscious statements in account books and similar records, from relationships we can discover among the works of art themselves, from inferences that may sometimes be drawn about the link between art and the political, intellectual, and social climate. There is only a limited number of instances in which we can hope to reconstruct the contemporary attitude toward a work of art without getting entangled in the vague generalities of *Geistesgeschichte*. Let us, then, try to be as specific as the present state of our knowledge permits.

In our quest of the new image of man in Renaissance art, we are primarily concerned with sculpture, for several good reasons. Most obvious is the matter of chronological priority: Early Renaissance art begins with sculpture—if I had to give specific dates, I should say between 1408 and 1416—while

Renaissance architecture makes its appearance in 1419 with Brunelleschi's designs for the Ospedale degli Innocenti and the Old Sacristy of S. Lorenzo, and painting has to await the emergence of Masaccio in the early 1420's. How did it happen that sculpture can claim this priority? We must, of course, give due credit to the individual genius of Donatello, but this genius could unfold only in the particular circumstances created by the spiritual climate of Florence during those decisive years. The new civic and republican humanism of Leonardo Bruni and his circle that made its appearance about 1400 gave birth to a vision of Florence as the modern counterpart of Periclean Athens,[2] and inspired a communal effort to beautify the city which in intensity and cost was entirely worthy of comparison with the art patronage of Athens during the later fifth century B.C. In Florence, this campaign meant first of all the completion of the unfinished artistic enterprises of earlier days; it began with the famous competition of 1401–3 for a second set of bronze doors for the Baptistery, then spread to the cathedral (the Porta della Mandorla, the façade, and the Campanile) and to the niches of Or San Michele. All these were sculptural tasks of great scope, challenging the best talent available. The most ambitious task of all, to be sure, was to build the long-projected dome of the cathedral, but this took so much deliberation that it did not get under way until 1420. Thus, for almost twenty years, the sculptors were the main beneficiaries of this great surge of communal art patronage. They had to work in a medieval setting, it is true, yet they soon managed to explode this framework and to create an image of man utterly unmedieval and attuned to the civic-patriotic humanism of the time.

Even if the painters had shared in the new art patronage from the start, I rather think the sculptors would have been in the van. For the image of man, in the most concrete, physical sense, is after all the central theme of sculpture anywhere and at any time; or at least of sculpture in the full meaning of the word, i.e., sculpture in the round and on a monumental scale, sculpture conceived as self-sufficient, free-standing statues rather than as the handmaiden of architecture. Sculpture thus defined had not been produced since the end of the Roman Empire— all medieval sculpture is "applied sculpture," whether or not it be physically in the round. Of course, most of medieval painting, too, is "applied," since it appears on surfaces such as walls, windows, altar frontals, or book pages, whose primary purpose was not to serve as carriers for images. Still, through the icons of Byzantine art, the tradition of ancient panel painting (that is, painting on surfaces that had no other purpose than to be painted on) survived throughout the Middle Ages and ultimately gave rise to the modern easel picture. The free-standing statue, on the other hand, survived neither in Byzantium nor in the medieval West (the last recorded instance is the statue of a Byzantine emperor made in the late eighth century). The reason is obvious: free-standing statues were "idols" par excellence. The early Christian fathers—I am thinking especially of a famous passage by Arnobius[3]—had expended great powers of rhetoric in trying to persuade their readers that the statues of the gods were not "real" but merely convenient depositories for the droppings of birds, yet the faith in the magic power of such statues would not die out. Only by placing sculpture in the service of the Church—and I mean this quite literally: by applying sculpture to church architecture— could the Middle Ages take the curse off monumental statuary. A statue standing unabashedly on its own two feet without being imprisoned by its architectural context was unthinkable.

Not that all free-standing statues of ancient times were destroyed as idols in the Middle Ages; we know that a small number of them survived in public view, such as the statues on the Lateran in Rome, which included the equestrian monument of Marcus Aurelius (rechristened Constantine the Great) and the Spinario, or Thorn Puller.[4] Occasionally such statues would turn up elsewhere as well. But no medieval artist dared to imitate them as free-standing figures; their poses or outlines were often borrowed, but always with a change of meaning and with a change from free to applied status. Clearly, these statues, especially if nude, retained some of their old magic; they were still looked upon as "the seats of demons," good or bad. Of the large number of medieval accounts attesting this fact,[5] let me cite just one, which I have chosen because it is so close in time to the Early Renaissance and can be linked to a fascinating visual example. About 1300—we do not know exactly when—there was discovered in Siena a nude Venus statue of the *pudica* type (the best-known example is the Medici Venus), inscribed with the name of Lysippus. The famous Greek sculptor, mentioned by Pliny and other Roman authors, had not been forgotten in the Middle Ages; the Sienese were delighted with their find, and after a while placed the figure atop the fountain in front of their city hall, a place of honor and responsibility that gave this particular statue something of the rank of a protective deity, like the *tyche* statues of ancient cities. It was thus quite natural that the Lysippean Venus should be held accountable for the fortunes of mid–fourteenth century Siena; and since these were largely misfortunes—we recall the plague of 1348—the city government decided, apparently in response to popular pressure, to get rid of the statue. A resolution passed by the city council in that year pronounced the figure *inhonestum* (indecent) but did not specify what should be done with it after its removal from the fountain. According to a somewhat later account, the Venus was broken into pieces and buried on Florentine soil, so that she might transfer her evil qualities to the enemy.[6] This Venus—or perhaps another one of the same type—appears on the Pisa Cathedral pulpit by Giovanni Pisano (Fig. 1), in the astonishing role of one of the cardinal virtues.[7] (Shortly before, Giovanni Pisano had been in charge of the sculptural program of Siena Cathedral and thus must have seen the Lysippean Venus if she was discovered while he was there.) This is a case unique in all of medieval art, and I suspect that in order to account for it we must assume that Giovanni Pisano wanted to take the curse off the Venus by giving her a place in the Christian scheme of things, symbolically speaking, and by putting her to use in the physical sense as well, since she is combined with four other figures that form one of the supports of the pulpit. Let us note, also, that he has been careful to deprive her of all sensuous appeal and to concentrate expression in the face; whereas in ancient nude statues, it is the body, rather than the face, that speaks to us most eloquently. (The loincloth, amusingly enough, is a modern addition.)

Against this background, it becomes understandable why the revival of the free-standing, self-sufficient statue was the first achievement of Early Renaissance art, an achievement that signals a radically unmedieval image of man. While ancient painting was barely known before the end of the Quattrocento, the free-standing statue was a primary symbol of that classical humanity whose modern heirs the Florentines of Leonardo Bruni's time had declared themselves to be. The other great visible symbol of the glories of antiquity was, of course, classical architecture, to which the young Brunelleschi devoted such painstaking study in Rome before he emerged, toward 1420, as the father of Renaissance architecture. But by then the new image of man in statuary form had already been coined. The new style in painting, that of Masaccio, needed both these precedents in order to become a reality.

Interestingly enough, sculpture maintains its priority even in the field of art theory, another great achievement of the Early Renaissance. Its founder, Leone Battista Alberti, was a humanist who came to the practice of art through his interest in art theory. He wrote three famous treatises, on sculpture, painting, and architecture; and that on sculpture has now been clearly established as the earliest, composed about 1430.[8] It is entitled, characteristically, *De statua,* and deals almost entirely with the free-standing statue. Moreover, Alberti is at pains to explain the origin of sculpture, while the origin of painting has little interest for him. His thesis, briefly stated, is that sculpture came into existence when some of our distant ancestors whose imaginations were so inclined became aware that certain tree trunks and clumps of earth suggested natural shapes (he implies the shape of human bodies). By modifying the tree trunks and clumps of earth, these people endeavored to make the resemblance more perfect, and eventually they learned how to achieve such a resemblance even if their material did not suggest it. Alberti's etiological theory, amazingly modern in its psychological implications, is not borrowed from the ancients.[9] It represents, I believe, an attempt to establish a solid basis for his definition of sculpture as free-standing statuary rather than as "applied sculpture." At the time he wrote down these thoughts, he probably had already become a friend of Donatello, the actual creator of the new image of man; and it may be no mere coincidence that the first life-size free-standing nude statue created since the end of antiquity, Donatello's bronze "David" (Fig. 2), dates from the same years in which *De statua* was composed.

Let us now trace the road from Giovanni Pisano's Gothic "Venus" to Donatello's bronze "David." It so happens that we can do this in some detail, and with enough testimony from contemporary records to lend conviction to our reading of the visual evidence. Our starting point is a pair of marble figures of 1408, the earliest known works—and very likely the first life-size statues—by Nanni di Banco and Donatello (Figs. 3 and 4). Today they are physically separated: Donatello's "David" is in the Museo Nazionale, Nanni's "Isaiah" in the cathedral. But they were clearly meant to be companion pieces, dependent on each other in their complementary body curves. These curves are still Gothic, and this is hardly surprising, since both figures were intended to crown the buttresses on the north side of Florence Cathedral.[10] Such statues—an entire cycle of prophets and apostles—had been planned long before, as we can see from the mid-fourteenth century representation of Florence Cathedral by Andrea da Firenze (Fig. 14); and all of these statues have the quality of curvilinear ornaments sprouting from the rigidly vertical buttresses to which they are anchored (and of which they are, in a sense, the outgrowth). Neither the "Isaiah" nor the "David" stands on its own two feet. They stand, rather, on their drapery, in the Gothic fashion. These folds are firmly united with the base, and both artists still rely on the material strength of the marble, not the inner balance of the bodies, to make their statues stand upright. Yet we also feel hints of an allegiance to ancient sculpture in the thrust-out right hip of the "Isaiah" and in his youthfulness, so different from the traditional image of Old Testament prophets in medieval art (who

are almost invariably old, and usually bearded.) Since the
"Isaiah" was commissioned some months before the "David,"
Nanni made the basic decision in choosing this youthful type;
Donatello had to follow his example, not only in the complementary body curve of his figure, but in representing David,
too, as a youth. He might have shown him as a young king.
Instead, he preferred the shepherd boy triumphing over Goliath.
We know of only one earlier image of the victorious youthful
David on a monumental scale, a fresco by Taddeo Gaddi of
the 1330's (Fig. 6), which provided the iconographic precedent
for Donatello's statue. Artistically, however, Donatello owes
nothing to Gaddi. His figure, less weighty and less aggressively
plastic than Nanni's, reflects the lithe elegance of Ghiberti's
style in both drapery and posture. We also note that the "David"
has a more assured stance than the "Isaiah," and that the mirror-
image symmetry of the two is not consistent in some details.
David's right hand, which ought to hold the prophet's scroll,
actually held the strap of the sling (the strap was of metal and
is now lost, but the drill holes for its attachment can still be
seen). As I have tried to show elsewhere, the symmetry of the
two statues was originally complete; such departures from it as
we observe today were introduced when Donatello recarved
parts of his figure in 1416.[11] As a matter of fact, we can still
trace the "ghost" of the scroll on the bare patch of drapery
over the right upper leg of the "David." Similarly, the odd bits
of drapery below the left hand originally extended as far down-
ward as the drapery over the right leg of the "Isaiah," largely
obscuring the left leg of the "David." Why these modifications?
Before we can answer this question, we must ask another: Why
weren't the two statues placed on their buttresses as intended?
The "Isaiah" actually reached his destination, but the statue

was taken down again after a short while because it was found too small to be effective at such a height; and the "David" was simply put in storage for the time being. This decision was made by the Opera del Duomo, the public body in charge of the cathedral workshop, and it was a revolutionary one, unthinkable before that time. Gothic cathedrals, north and south of the Alps, abound with statuary at all levels from the ground, but the scale of these figures is not governed by their distance from the beholder. After all, they were made *ad majorem gloriam dei,* so that their visibility to human eyes could not be a determining factor. Yet that is exactly what the decision of the cathedral workshop implies with respect to the "Isaiah" and the "David." Two years later, the Opera commissioned Donatello to make another prophet for one of the buttresses, a Joshua of brick and plaster, which was intended as a temporary figure, to be replaced by a marble version if its size proved to be right.[12] That statue, demolished in the seventeenth century because of its poor condition, was no less than eighteen feet tall, or three times the height of the "David" of 1408! Its effect must have been dramatic—it came to be regarded as one of Donatello's chief claims to fame[13]—but the task of replacing it with a marble version and of completing the entire series on the same scale was overwhelming. We shall return to this problem shortly. For the moment, let us note that in Florence, about 1410, we find the first colossal statue since antiquity, inspired not by the classical precedents then known, such as the remains of the colossal statue of Constantine on view at the Lateran, but by a thoroughly modern consideration, the eye measure that demanded such a huge scale because of the distance of the statue from the beholder.[14]

PLATE I

Fig. 1. (left).—Giovanni Pisano. "Virtue." Detail of the marble pulpit, Pisa Cathedral. 1302–10. (Photograph: Alinari.)

Fig. 2 (right).—Donatello. Bronze "David." Museo Nazionale, Florence. ca. 1430–32. (Photograph: Alinari-Brogi.)

PLATE II

FIG. 3 *(left).*—Nanni di Banco. "Isaiah." Florence Cathedral. 1408. (Photograph: Alinari.)

FIG. 4 *(right).*—Donatello. Marble "David." Museo Nazionale, Florence. 1408; modified 1416 (Photograph: Alinari-Brogi.)

PLATE III

FIG. 5 (left).—Donatello. "St. Mark." Or San Michele, Florence. 1411–13. (Photograph: Alinari-Brogi.)

FIG. 6 (right).—Taddeo Gaddi. "David." Baroncelli Chapel, S. Croce, Florence. ca. 1330–35. (Photograph: Alinari.)

PLATE IV

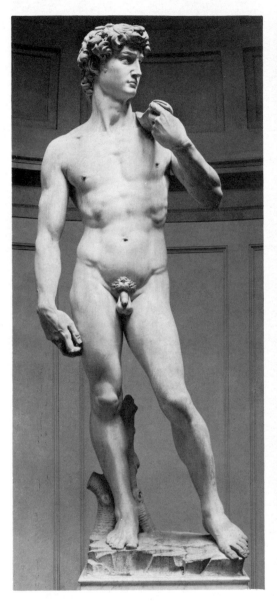

Fig. 7 *(left).*—Michelangelo. "David." Accademia, Florence. 1501–4. (Photograph: Alinari.)

Fig. 8 *(right).*—Donatello. "St. George." Museo Nazionale, Florence. *ca.* 1416. (Photograph Alinari-Brogi.)

PLATE V

Fig. 9 —Nanni di Banco. "Four Saints" ("Quattro Coronati"). Or San Michele, Florence. *ca.*
1410–14. (Photograph: Alinari.)

PLATE VI

Fig. 10 (left).—Donatello. "Beardless Prophet." Museo dell'Opera del Duomo, Florence. 1416–18. (Photograph: Alinari-Brogi.)

Fig. 11 (right).—Donatello. "Bearded Prophet." Museo dell'Opera del Duomo, Florence. 1418–20. (Photograph: Alinari-Brogi.)

PLATE VII

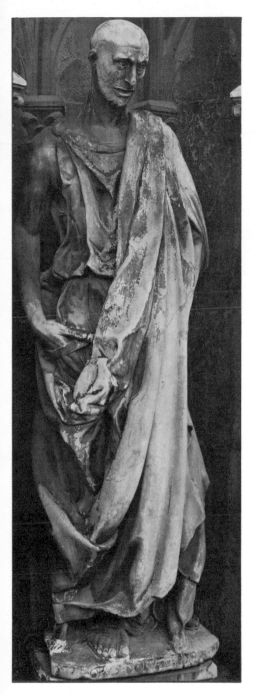

Fig. 12 (*left*).—Donatello. "Prophet" ("Zuccone"). Museo dell'Opera del Duomo, Florence. 1423–25. (Photograph: Alinari-Brogi.)

Fig. 13 (*right*).—Donatello. "Prophet" ("Jeremiah"). Museo dell'Opera del Duomo, Florence. 1427–35. (Photograph: Alinari-Brogi.)

PLATE VIII

Fig. 14.—Florence Cathedral, detail from Andrea da Firenze, "The Church Militant and Triumphant." Spanish Chapel, S. Maria Novella, Florence. 1365–68. (Photograph: Alinari-Anderson.)

PLATE IX

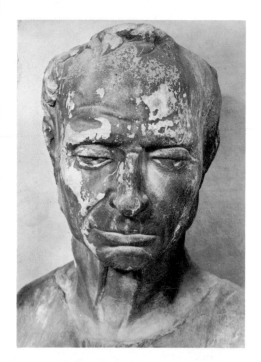

Fig. 15 (above).—Detail of Fig. 10. (Photograph: Alinari-Brogi.)

Fig. 16 (below).—Roman portrait. Museo Vaticano, Rome. ca. 50 B.C. (From *Roman Portraits* [Phaidon Edition; New York: Oxford University Press, 1940].)

PLATE X

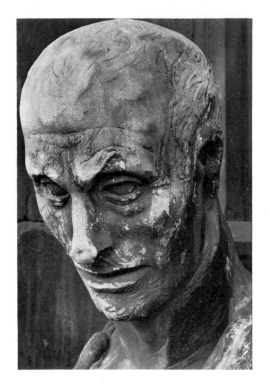

Fig. 17 *(left)*.—Detail of Fig. 12. (Photograph: Alinari-Brogi.)
Fig. 18 *(right)*.—So-called "Trajanus Decius". Museo Capitolino, Rome. Third century A.D.

PLATE XI

Fig. 19.—Detail of Fig. 13. (Photograph: Alinari-Brogi.)

PLATE XII

Fig. 20.—Detail of Fig. 2. (Photograph: Alinari-Brogi.)

PLATE XIII

F<small>IG</small>. 21.—"Head of Antinous." Museo Archeologico, Florence. *ca.* 125 A.D. (Photograph: Alinari.)

PLATE XIV

Fig. 22 (left).—Donatello. "Angel with Tambourine." Staatliche Museen, Berlin-Dahlem. 1429.
Fig. 23 (right).—Michelangelo. "David." Pen drawing, Cabinet des Dessins, Louvre, Paris. 1501.

PLATE XV

Fig. 24.—Bernardo Rossellino. Tomb of Leonardo Bruni. S. Croce, Florence. *ca.* 1445–50. (Photograph: Alinari.)

PLATE XVI

Fig. 25.—Doorway of the Pantheon, Rome. *ca.* 115–25 A.D. (Photograph: Alinari.)

Meanwhile, however, a most interesting fate awaited the "David" of 1408. In 1416, the city government urgently requested its transfer from the storerooms of the cathedral to the Palazzo Vecchio, the city hall, where it was placed against a wall in one of the great public rooms. We do not know who conceived this idea or what particular occasion prompted the request. An informed guess, however, would be that the suggestion came from one of the humanists prominent in the city government, such as Leonardo Bruni, and that the occasion was some anticipated visit by an important political figure whom the city fathers wanted to impress, symbolically, with that Florentine resolution in the face of external threats which had enabled the city to resist Giangaleazzo Visconti at the turn of the century. That such was indeed the new role of the "David" is evident from the inscription attached to the statue once it was installed in the Palazzo Vecchio: "To those who bravely fight for the fatherland, the gods will lend aid even against the most terrible foes." The plural, "gods," is especially piquant in relation to an Old Testament hero; but Donatello had endowed the head of his David with a victory wreath from the very start and thus given him something of the cast of a classical victor. Now that the statue had become a civic-patriotic symbol, the victory aspect had to be emphasized, and it was for that purpose that Donatello recarved some portions of it. He removed the prophet's scroll as superfluous, and exposed the left leg to stress the assurance—indeed, the insouciance—of the hero's stance. One is almost tempted to describe this pose as a precocious instance of *sprezzatura,* that studied lack of conscious effort which played so important a part in Cinquecento art theory.[15]

In exposing the left leg of his David, Donatello superimposed his style of 1416 on a figure carved eight years before. It was these eight years that made all the difference; for in the meantime, he had re-created the free-standing statue. The occasion was again one of the great communal artistic campaigns, the filling of the empty niches on the exterior of the church of the Florentine guilds, Or San Michele. The plan had been conceived many years before, but nothing much had been done about it until 1410, when the city government enjoined all the guilds to provide statues for their niches or forfeit the right to do so. Here, too, Nanni di Banco and Donatello worked side by side, and again a comparison of their work is instructive. Nanni's earliest niche holds the Quattro Coronati, patron saints of the stonecarvers (Fig. 9). Since these four martyrs, whose individual identity is obscure, formed a unit, the artist had to fill the niche with four statues rather than a single figure. Their style, especially that of the second, third, and fourth figure from the left, is strikingly reminiscent of classical statues—far more so than is the "Isaiah" of 1408. Still, Nanni could not yet free himself of the medieval habit of thinking in terms of "applied" sculpture: each statue is placed against a pilaster, so that it functions like the statues attached to columns on the jambs of Gothic church portals. And, in order to stress the dependence of the figures on their architectural setting, Nanni has taken a bite out of the niche floor, so to speak, reducing it to a semicircular ledge (and thus pinning the statues against the pilasters). About the same time, 1411–13, Donatello filled the niche of the linen weavers with a St. Mark (Fig. 5).[16] Here, at one stroke, we find ourselves in the Early Renaissance, although the niche itself is no less Gothic than that of the Quattro Coronati. This statue no longer depends on its setting for support; it could stand with perfect poise and assurance anywhere. Unlike the earlier figures discussed here, it sustains itself on its own two legs, displaying that complex internal body balance, or *contrapposto,* familiar in classical statues (which in every other respect it resembles far less than do the Quattro Coronati). It is the first statue since antiquity constructed on a vertical line—the axis of gravity—linking the top of the head with the heel of the "engaged leg" (the leg carrying the main weight of the body), and the first statue since antiquity that can be said to have been conceived as a nude body subsequently covered with clothing: the drapery now no longer plays its own rhythmic game of curvilinear folds, but follows—and thus conveys to the beholder—the body forms underneath. This, then, is the earliest post-medieval image of man we know, an image of the human body conceived as a functional, articulated mechanism sustained by muscular power. Donatello makes this clear, apart from everything we have observed so far, by placing the statue on a cushion (the earliest case of its kind), an elastic support that yields under the weight of the body, with the engaged leg causing a deeper imprint than the free leg. What device could be better calculated to remove the flavor of "stoniness" that still clings to the two prophets of 1408 and the Quattro Coronati?

In his next niche statue, the "St. George" of *ca.* 1416, carved for the armorers' guild (Fig. 8),[17] Donatello took a further step. The figure now begins to protrude beyond the front plane of the niche, because the engaged leg (the left one in this instance) is placed forward, so as to endow the statue with a sense of alertness, of readiness for combat, or *prontezza* (as the artist's contemporaries called it).[18] With this physical tension goes a new psychological alertness, a strained gaze from under knitted eyebrows—our first encounter with that calculated dominance over the beholder which, in the hands of Michelangelo, became the quality called *terribilità* (see Fig. 7). Had Donatello been called upon at this point to produce a free-standing statue for the center of a courtyard or public square, he would have been fully capable of doing so. Public art patronage, however, did not yet afford him this opportunity. The closest he could come to it was to transfer something of the vigor of his "St. George" to the "David" of 1408 in the Palazzo Vecchio.

Until now Donatello, unlike Nanni di Banco, had not introduced any overt references to classical sculpture into his work. The *contrapposto* of the "St. Mark" reflects the stance of an ancient statue in a very general way, but it was only the principle, not the external appearance, that the artist had taken over. This situation was to change dramatically from about 1416 onward: Nanni di Banco, in his last work, the "Assumption of the Virgin," above the Porta della Mandorla of Florence Cathedral (*ca.* 1418–21), relinquished his classicism and achieved an utterly novel dynamic style,[19] while Donatello during these years betrayed an ever keener interest in ancient sculpture. After the basic conquests of the "St. Mark" and the "St. George," he needed the inspiration of ancient art in order to arrive at a full definition of his new image of man. His main project of the decade following the "St. George" was a series of prophet statues for the Campanile of Florence Cathedral, a commission he shared with some lesser sculptors who followed his lead.[20] The Gothic niches of the Campanile were far more confining than were those of Or San Michele. Since they were not only tall and narrow but high above the street level, Donatello could not repeat what he had done in the case of the "St. George," i.e., let the statues protrude from their niches in order to establish their rapport with the beholder. The four figures I shall discuss show him groping for a solution and finding it, triumphantly, in the end. Although these statues are amply documented, their individual identities remain in doubt; apart from one instance, the records refer to them simply as "prophets" without giving their names. We can thus call the earliest of the series only "the beardless prophet" (Figs. 10 and 15). The statue shows the conventional medieval type—an old man in long garments displaying a large scroll—except for the head, which is its most impressive feature. This clean-shaven, thoroughly individualized face with its sharply cut lines clearly reflects a republican Roman portrait such as the specimen in Fig. 16. A strange and incongruous union! Donatello must have felt this, for his second prophet (Fig. 11) represents a different alternative: the bearded head is not portraitlike at all—it recalls the type of the "St. Mark" —but the whole concept of the figure no longer suggests the traditional prophet type. The scroll has almost disappeared; it is rolled up and held in the left hand, whose main function is to support the right arm, which reaches up to the chin. This gesture, here meant to convey deep meditation, is thoroughly familiar in classical art as a gesture of mourning. There are countless examples of it in funerary sculpture and in representations of captive barbarians.[21] Donatello interpreted it as expressing concentrated thought; his aim must have been to give this prophet the appearance of an ancient philosopher, and he has come astonishingly close to matching the spirit, if not the detail, of classical statues of philosophers (which, in all likelihood, were not known to him). The third prophet (Figs. 12 and 17), nicknamed "Zuccone" (bald-head), is an intensified synthesis of the previous two. The scroll is now tucked away beneath the right hand, the great mantle descending from the left shoulder strongly suggests a Roman toga, and the sleeveless undergarment is just as obviously of classical inspiration. In the fascinating ugliness of the head, we find qualities reflecting the two great periods of Roman portraiture, the republican and the third century A.D. (compare Figs. 16, 18). Here, then, is an integrated, and radical, reinterpretation of a biblical prophet. But what thoughts was the "Zuccone" meant to evoke in the contemporary beholder's mind? Clearly he is not a philosopher like his meditative predecessor. Instead of being withdrawn into the world of his thoughts, he seems to address the crowd down below—note that his mouth is partly open. This impression is recorded in the Renaissance anecdote that Donatello, while at work on the "Zuccone," used to shout at him, "Speak, speak, or the plague take you!" The statue thus suggests a figure from the world of antiquity, but a figure devoid of idealization or classical balance. What was the type that Donatello wanted to revive and to equate with the prophets of the Old Testament? There can be only one answer: the "Zuccone" is the biblical counterpart of a Roman republican *rhetor,* a kind of Cato preaching civic virtue, liberty, and patriotic fervor. He is, in short, the tangible embodiment of the historic vision of Leonardo Bruni and his circle, with its exaltation of the free cities of ancient Etruria, of republican Rome, of the city republic of Athens. In the guise of a religious subject, Donatello has created a monument to the political *ethos* of Florentine humanism. No wonder the statue won lasting popularity almost at once, a popularity reflected in the large number of anecdotes that came to cluster around it. The final member of the series, later dubbed "Jeremiah," [22] repeats the same idea; because of the exposed right shoulder, he comes even closer to the appearance of an ancient hero, and his forensic spirit is equally pronounced (Figs. 13

and 19). The two figures were always linked in the popular imagination of Florence. Characteristically enough, that they represented biblical prophets seems to have been forgotten soon after they were put on public display. From the early Cinquecento onward, the sources refer to them as portrait statues of Francesco Soderini and Giovanni di Barduccio Cherichini. This, of course, is nonsense, factually speaking, but the story fits the character of the statues very well indeed. It must have arisen during the brief interval between the expulson of the Medici and their return, when the city was governed once more according to its traditional republican institutions, under a Gonfaloniere who was a descendant of the Francesco Soderini supposedly portrayed by the "Zuccone" or the "Jeremiah." Moreover, Francesco Soderini and Giovanni di Barduccio Cherichini both were conspicuously involved in the banishment of Cosimo de' Medici from Florence in 1433. Three-quarters of a century later, their anti-Medicean politics earned them the status of heroes of republican virtue, and identification with Donatello's statues.

Discounting the gigantic "Joshua" of *ca.* 1410 (which, apart from its size, probably did not look very different from the "David" of 1408), Donatello by the end of the third decade of the century had not yet produced a statue that was free-standing in fact as well as in spirit. This, it seems, became possible only about 1430. At that time the artist received two commissions for such works, one public and one private. The former, unfortunately, is lost: it was a figure of "Dovizia" (Wealth), a female personification analogous to Fortuna or Tyche, atop a column in the center of the Mercato Vecchio, the old market square of Florence. In the seventeenth century it was replaced by a baroque statue, since it had been badly damaged by wind and weather (the material was either marble or limestone). We do not even have an adequate visual record of its appearance; it was placed too high above the ground for anybody to sketch it in detail, and general views of the old market give us only a vague suggestion of what the "Dovizia" looked like. From contemporary records, however, we know that the figure enjoyed great popularity, and that it must have been done about the same time as the Prato pulpit, or *ca.* 1430. The column form was, of course, the classic way of displaying a free-standing statue, a method well remembered in the Middle Ages, for there were countless representations of pagan idols on columns in medieval art.[23]

The other commission, from an unknown but surely private source, produced the famous bronze "David" (Fig. 2), the first free-standing bronze statue since antiquity and the first life-size free-standing nude.[24] Its pose contains reminiscences of the "David" of 1408, but the most daring—and still rather enigmatic—aspect of the figure is its nudity. It has been accounted for in a number of ways; iconographically, it could be the nudity of humility,[25] or the nudity of the "athlete of virtue," an early Christian concept identifying the athletic contests of Greece with the quest for Christian virtue.[26] Be that as it may, the most striking fact about the bronze "David" is not that it is nude but that it is nude in the classical sense; Donatello here recaptures the full sensuous beauty of the nude body, the element that had been so conspicuously absent from Giovanni Pisano's copy of the Lysippean Venus. It is part of this classical quality of the bronze "David" that the body is more eloquent than the face, which by Donatello's standards seems oddly impersonal and emotionally neutral (Fig. 20). It reminds us of the Antinous heads in Roman art (Fig. 21). Perhaps it is no mere chance that Hadrian's favorite, too, was often represented nude, although Donatello probably did not know such statues. There is yet another likely motivation for the nudity of the bronze "David": its date coincides with that of Alberti's treatise *De statua,* which deals at length with the structure and proportions of the nude body.[27]

Much as one would like to think that Donatello actually saw (and adapted to his and Alberti's conception) an ancient life-size statue of a nude youth, the classical inspiration of the bronze "David" probably reached Donatello by a less direct path, through small bronze statuettes of Etruscan or Roman manufacture. These, we know, were available and highly appreciated in the Early Renaissance, before excavations in Rome during the sixteenth century brought to light ancient marble figures of monumental scale in such quantity as to redefine the Renaissance appreciation of classical sculpture. The immediate ancestors of the bronze "David" in Donatello's *oeuvre* are the three bronze statuettes of nude angel *putti* which Donatello did in 1429 for the central tabernacle of the font in the baptistery of Siena Cathedral.[28] The finest of them (Fig. 22) was stolen and is now in the Berlin Museum. From the appearance of this enchanting little figure—its height is fourteen inches—we would never surmise that it was made as a piece of architectual sculpture in miniature. Completely free and balanced in movement, turning on its base with spontaneous *joie de vivre,* it has all the unself-conscious, natural state of nudity that is the heritage of the classical *putto.* There can be little doubt, even though we have no matching example, that its source of inspiration was an ancient small bronze. Here the nudity, being that of a child, is non-controversial, while that of the "David" undoubtedly needed justification along the lines I suggested above.

We do not know the original location of the bronze "David." The statue enters the known records only in the 1460's, when it stood in the courtyard of the Medici Palace in Florence. After the expulsion of the Medici in 1494, it came to share the fate of the marble "David"; transferred to the courtyard of the Palazzo Vecchio, it, too, became a public monument, a civic symbol like the earlier figure. At that time the bronze "David" so impressed the French ambassador that he requested in 1501 to have a replica made and offered to pay the cost of the casting.[29] It was in response to this wish that the young Michelangelo made his first "David," a bronze statue, now lost, which followed the lines of Donatello's. We know its appearance from one of the master's drawings (Fig. 23).

What had happened, meanwhile, to the project of those colossal statues for the buttresses of Florence Cathedral? After Donatello's provisional "Joshua" of *ca.* 1410, he and Brunelleschi were paid for some small-scale models,[30] but that is the last we hear of the matter for several decades. A marble block of the right size was eventually procured, but no Florentine sculptor of the later Quattrocento was capable of carving an eighteen-foot statue from it, and the attempt was abandoned once more. Finally, in 1501, the cathedral authorities turned this huge block over to Michelangelo, who made it into his famous marble "David" (Fig. 7), the companion or replacement of Donatello's "Joshua" on the north side of the cathedral. Yet, like the "David" of 1408, Michelangelo's "David" never reached its intended location. It, too, was taken away from the cathedral authorities by municipal action and erected in front of the

Palazzo Vecchio—the third, and most impressive, civic-patriotic symbol of the Florentine republic.[31] Artistically, too, it sums up the entire long development that began in 1408, combining the colossal size of the "Joshua," the nudity of the bronze "David," the conversion from a religious to a civic purpose first experienced by Donatello's marble "David" in 1416, and the *prontezza*, the agressive alertness, of the "St. George."

In closing, we must refer once more to Leonardo Bruni, the most important of the intellectual godfathers of the new image of man. It is an oddly symbolic circumstance that Bruni's tomb in S. Croce (Fig. 24) should be the earliest complete formulation of a Renaissance funerary monument and the model for countless later ones. The new image of man that we saw emerging in the statues of Donatello also demanded a new image of man in relation to death, but the latter emerged only in 1445–50, while Donatello was absent from Florence.[32] Had he been available at the time of Bruni's death in March 1444, he surely would have been asked to carve the great humanist's tomb; under the circumstances, the commission fell to a younger and lesser master, Bernardo Rossellino, only recently established in Florence. His chief qualification, it seems, was that he had worked in Arezzo, Bruni's home town, and thus was well known to the Aretines, who took a great interest in the monument honoring their most distinguished native son.[33] The importance of the Bruni tomb rests less on the quality of its sculpture than on the concept of the entire design; and this we cannot credit to Rossellino alone. He must have had at least the advice of a far more important artist, charged by the Florentine authorities with the task of seeing to it that the Bruni tomb was fully worthy of the deceased. This man, it has been suggested, was Leone Battista Alberti, and I believe this hypothesis, although

generally disregarded nowadays, has a good deal of plausibility.[34] Bruni himself had no faith in funerary monuments.
In his will, he requested burial in S. Croce under a plain marble
slab. We know from a famous letter he wrote in 1429–30 to
Poggio Bracciolini about the tomb of another humanist, Bartolommeo Aragazzi, that he thought nobody with any faith in
his own fame should want a conspicuous tomb, since deeds
alone insure everlasting memory.[35] Yet it is exactly the idea of
fame that dominates the design of the Bruni tomb and distinguishes it from all its predecessors. Medieval tombs were
based on the juxtaposition of time and eternity: man's fleeting
presence on this earth as against the destiny of his immortal
soul. The former aspect is conveyed by the effigy of the deceased
on its bier and the inscription stating his name, his rank or
office, and the date of his death; the latter aspect by religious
imagery such as the Resurrection of Christ, the Man of Sorrows,
Christ in Majesty, the Madonna, and so forth. Of all this, there
is barely a hint in the Bruni tomb; the only religious element
is the Madonna with angels in the lunette, which certainly
does not dominate the monument as a whole. There is, to be
sure, the effigy, but Bruni looks as if he were peacefully slum-
bering, and various details record the state funeral specially
arranged for Bruni. According to the description by Vespasiano
da Bisticci,[36] it was a ceremony "in the manner of the ancients,"
with the corpse dressed in the same silk robe Bruni had worn
in life, and with a copy of his famous *History of Florence* placed
in his hands. (That is clearly what the heavy tome on the
chest of the effigy is intended to represent.) The climax of the
funeral was the crowning of Bruni's head with a laurel wreath;
and that, too, is shown in the effigy. Moreover, the inscription,
composed by Carlo Marsuppini, Bruni's successor as secretary

of the republic, conspicuously omits all the usual data: we learn from it neither the last name of the deceased nor his station in life and the date of his death. All it tells us is: "After Leonardo's passing, History grieves, Eloquence is silent, and the Muses, 'tis said, Greek and Latin alike, cannot restrain their tears." The tablet on which these words are inscribed is held by two winged genii, rather than by angels, and two more such genii, nude this time, support the family coat of arms above the lunette. It seems to have escaped attention that the framing architecture, which unites all these sculptural features so harmoniously, is also meant to convey a message to the beholder. Tombs in niches had been customary for a long time; what is new here is the shape of the niche and its framework—two classical pilasters supporting an equally classical entablature, above which rises a round arch. There is a specific source in ancient architecture for this design, and its choice is highly significant: the doorway of the Pantheon in Rome as seen from the interior of that structure (Fig. 25). The motif was surely meant to be recognized by the contemporary beholder, for in the eyes of the Quattrocento the Pantheon was a uniquely famous monument combining the highest aspirations of both antiquity and Christianity. To Alberti, the Pantheon represented the perfect temple and thus also the perfect church. (In his treatise on architecture, completed by 1452, he strenuously argues in favor of church plans based on the circle and against the traditional basilican plan, declaring basilican churches imperfect because in antiquity the basilica had not been a religious type of building.)[37] The Pantheon, moreover, was dedicated to all the immortals—the gods of old as well as the martyrs of the Christian faith. (In the early Middle Ages, it was consecrated as S. Maria ad Martyres, and the remains of martyrs were gathered there by the wagon load from the catacombs.) The archway of the Bruni tomb thus suggests to the beholder that Bruni is about to enter the realm of immortality, in both the classical and the Christian sense. The moment of Bruni's passing from this earth, when his mortal remains are still above ground but surrounded by the accoutrements of undying fame—the book, the wreath, the inscription—has thus been eternalized by showing the effigy, as it were, on the threshold of the Pantheon. The medieval juxtaposition of time and eternity, of body and soul, has lost its force. That this concept (though not its artistic execution) originated with Alberti seems likely not only in view of what he says about the Pantheon in his architectural treatise but also because the doorway of the Pantheon was one of his favorite motifs as a church architect: he used it for the main portal of S. Maria Novella in Florence and again, on an even grander scale, as the central feature of the façade of S. Andrea in Mantua. By introducing the motif into the design of tombs, Alberti accomplished two objectives at once. He gave the Renaissance tomb a new, unmedieval significance, and he raised it from the level of "church furniture" to that of monumental architecture, endowing it with a stability and grandeur fully expressive of its "fame-centered" meaning.

1. Cf. Anthony Blunt, *Artistic Theory in Italy, 1480–1600* (Oxford, 1956), pp. 97 f., on the influence of Baldassare Castiglione's *Cortegiano,* as well as the illuminating paper, "Maniera as an Aesthetic Ideal," by John Shearman, in *Studies in Western Art, Acts of the Twentieth International Congress of the History of Art,* II, Princeton, 1963, pp. 200 ff.

2. See Hans Baron, *The Crisis of the Early Renaissance* (Princeton, N.J., 1955), and the same author's *Humanistic and Political Literature in Florence and Venice* (Cambridge, Mass., 1955).

3. *Adversus Gentes,* VI, 16; cf. also Clement of Alexandria, *Cohortatio ad Gentes,* Migne, *Patrologia Graeca,* VIII, cols. 155 ff.

4. See W. S. Heckscher, *s. v.* "Dornauszieher," in *Reallexikon zur deutschen Kunstgeschichte* (1955), IV, cols. 289 ff., and the literature cited there.

5. Cf. Julius v. Schlosser, *Leben und Meinungen des florentinischen Bildners Lorenzo Ghiberti* (Basel, 1941), p. 156. For the statue of Mars on the Ponte Vecchio in Florence, destroyed in 1333, see Giovanni Villani, *Historie Fiorentine*, XI, i; for the imperial equestrian monument nicknamed the Regisole in Pavia, see Hans Kauffman, *Donatello* (Berlin, 1935), pp. 134, 236 n. 413; and Ludwig H. Heydenreich, "Marc Aurel und Regisole," in *Festschrift für Erich Meyer* (Hamburg, 1959), pp. 146 ff. (with exhaustive bibliography).

6. For a detailed account, see Schlosser, *loc. cit.*

7. The choice seems to be between Temperance and Chastity. The arguments have been summarized in Erwin Panofsky, *Studies in Iconology* (New York, 1939 and 1962) p. 157.

8. See H. W. Janson, "The 'Image Made by Chance' in Renaissance Thought," in *De artibus opuscula XL: Essays in Honor of Erwin Panofsky* (New York, 1961), pp. 254 ff.

9. Cf. Janson, *op. cit.*

10. A detailed account of the two statues and the documents relating to them is given in H. W. Janson, *The Sculpture of Donatello* (Princeton, N.J., 1957), II, 3 ff. (hereinafter referred to as Janson, *Donatello*).

11. Janson, *Donatello*, 3 ff.

12. Giovanni Poggi, *Il Duomo di Firenze* (Berlin, 1909), nos. 414–21; and Janson, *Donatello*, pp. 4 f., 14 f., 226.

13. The well-known physician and scholar Giovanni Chellini recorded in his *Libro debitori creditori e ricordanze* that on August 27, 1456, he had treated Donatello, "singulare e precipuo maestro" who had done the eighteen-foot-tall giant above one of the chapels of the cathedral. That Chellini should have chosen this figure from the multitude of Donatello's works in Florence suggests that he regarded it as the master's greatest feat. The *Libro* is preserved in the Saminiati Archives at the Università Bocconi in Milan; the passage cited above was published by Aldo de Maddalena in *Annales: Économies, Sociétés, Civilisations*, XIV, (1959), 743. Cf. H. W. Janson, "Giovanni Chellini's Libro . . . ," in *Studien zur toskanischen Kunst, Festschrift für Ludwig Heinrich Heydenreich*, Munich, 1964, pp. 131–38.

14. The term "colossal" here implies not merely that a statue is significantly larger than life-size but also that the beholder must experience it as gigantic (as the Florentines evidently did Donatello's "Joshua"). Erwin Panofsky's generalization (in *Renaissance and Renascences in Western Art* [Stockholm, 1960], p. 28 f.) that "in a Gothic cathedral . . . none of the statues is appreciably over lifesized" because medieval architecture is "epanthropic" (i.e., scaled with reference to the absolute size of the human body, while ancient architecture is dimensioned in analogy to the relative proportions of the human figure) is valid in terms of the beholder's subjective experience if not of objective measurement. At Reims Cathedral, the jamb statues—the only ones within the beholder's direct physical range—are indeed

"not appreciably over lifesized," but others, at greater distance from the ground, are over twelve feet tall. Yet these do not strike the beholder as gigantic unless he sees them at ground level, removed from their architectural context (one such figure, the "Ecclesia," was thus displayed in the summer of 1962 in the Louvre, as part of an exhibition devoted to French cathedrals). Panofsky's claim thus remains true in principle. It certainly serves to dramatize the fundamental, and as yet insufficiently explored, fact that the medieval sculptor labored under limitations not imposed on the medieval painter. Perhaps we must look for the legitimate successors to the colossal statues of Roman emperors, not in medieval sculpture, but in painting; for the Pantocrator mosaics on the domes and apses of Byzantine churches, and the standing saints of stained glass in the clerestory windows of Chartres and Bourges, are surely intended to be experienced as colossal images. In contrast, medieval sculptured figures more than twice life-size would seem to occur only under very special circumstances that permitted a suspension of the ordinary rules. Such a case is the "St. Christopher," more than eighteen feet tall, on the façade of the Cathedral of Gemona (Venezia Giulia), carved by Giovanni Griglio and dated 1331; St. Christopher, after all, was a giant, hence the statute was not really "over life sized." Moreover, he was the special patron of travelers, who believed that a glance at an image of the saint would protect them from mishaps for the rest of that day, so that the huge size of the Gemona figure appears doubly justified (no passerby could miss it). The Roland statues in certain North German towns may owe their large size to similar considerations.

15, On *sprezzatura,* see the references cited in note 1, above, and in Janson, *Donatello,* pp. 36, 40.

16. For a detailed account, see Janson, *Donatello,* pp. 16–21.

17. For a detailed account, see *ibid.,* pp. 23–32.

18. The earliest use of the term in praise of the "St. George" is found in Filarete's *Trattato dell'architettura,* written 1451–64 (edited by Wolfgang v. Oettingen [Vienna, 1890]), p. 622. See Janson, *Donatello,* p. 24.

19. Cf. H. W. Janson, *History of Art* (New York, 1962), p. 306, and "Nanni di Banco's Assumption of the Virgin on the Porta della Mandorla," in *Studies in Western Art, op. cit.,* pp. 98 ff.

20. For a detailed account, see Janson, *Donatello,* pp. 33–41.

21. Cf. Dorothy C. Shorr, "The Mourning Virgin and Saint John," *Art Bulletin,* XXII (1940), 61 ff., for the use of the gesture in ancient art.

22. In the cathedral records, Donatello's last Campanile prophet is called a Habakkuk; none of the documents or sources mention a Jeremiah, although that name is inscribed on the scroll of the statue which, for reasons of style, seems the latest of the series. There is reason to believe that the inscription was added by a later hand, probably in 1464. See Janson, *Donatello,* p. 39.

23. See Werner Haftmann, *Das italienische Säulenmonument* (Leipzig, 1939), pp. 139 ff., and Kauffmann, *op. cit.,* pp. 41 ff.

24. For a detailed account, see Janson, *Donatello,* pp. 77–86.

25. As maintained by Kauffmann, *op. cit.*, pp. 159 ff.

26. See Colin Eisler, "The Athlete of Virtue," *De artibus opuscula XL: Essays in Honor of Erwin Panofsky*, pp. 82–97.

27. A few years later, the publication of Alberti's treatise on painting evoked a similarly immediate response in the relief compositions of Donatello and Ghiberti; see Janson, *Donatello*, pp. 129 ff., and the literature cited there.

28. For a detailed account, see *ibid.*, pp. 65–75.

29. See *ibid.*, p. 78.

30. See Poggi, *op. cit.*, no. 423.

31. See Janson, *Donatello*, pp. 198 f.

32. Donatello worked in Padua from late 1443 to 1453. For the circumstances of his departure and return, see *ibid.*, pp. 147 ff., 188 f.

33. For the most recent discussion of the Bruni tomb, and a critical summary of earlier literature, see John Pope-Hennessy, *Italian Renaissance Sculpture* (London and New York, 1958), pp. 297 f.

34. Pope-Hennessy, *loc. cit.*, rejects it without argument.

35. Cited, in part, by Pope-Hennessy, *op. cit.*, p. 41.

36. Summarized by Pope-Hennessy, *ibid.*, p. 297.

37. For Alberti's theories, and their philosophical background, see Rudolf Wittkower, *Architectural Principles in the Age of Humanism* (rev. ed.; London, 1962), *passim*.

PAOLO TOSCANELLI
AND HIS FRIENDS

By

Giorgio de Santillana

THE RENAISSANCE remains a mysterious thing. It is an age of hazy outlines, illuminated by flashes of passionate affirmation, an epoch of conflict and contradiction, an epoch in which there is the Council of Trent as well as Erasmus and Montaigne, in which the new astronomy comes into collision with the all-powerful, and advancing, astrology, in which the renascence of mathematics allies itself with the resurgence of magic. The sixteenth century is unbelievably far from us by its presuppositions, its mental habits, its superstitious respect for ancient authority, by the very structure of its intelligence which was ready to accept not only belief but knowledge *ex auditu,* from hearsay. Something of this bewildering texture begins to appear in detail when we bring into focus men and activities hitherto barely known.

I should like to discuss an enigmatic personage of the fifteenth century who was called by his contemporaries Master Paul the physician. He was a quiet man. We know so little of his life, his thought, and his personality that we have to reconstruct them by hints and clues. He is, nonetheless, the invisible knot that ties together a number of prodigious personalities—the very men who may be said to have invented the Renaissance and to have started the scientific revolution.

Not too much has been written about him, because so little is known. About fifty years ago, a big book was written about him by Uzielli which contained everything, including what is disputable, and built him up into a very important figure indeed. Then later, in his great *History of Magic and Experimental Science,* Lynn Thorndike undertook rather acidly to cut down to size the "Toscanelli myth," as he called it. And then in 1961, a new study came out by Eugenio Garin, the well-known Florentine scholar, in his *Renaissance Studies,* which is really a brief reappraisal. Garin's authority as a cultural historian stands so high that it is rather chancy to go and revise the question just after him. On the other hand, there is without doubt a slight slant to his thought because he is also an authority on the intellectual history of modern Italy: his strong progressive convictions have developed into a penchant for historical materialism, quite understandable if you have to deal with certain overripe subjects. And so Garin presents Toscanelli the technician and businessman, the healthy representative of the dynamic Florentine entrepreneur class which was reaching at that time its apogee. Surely, in fact, one may wonder why Garin did not bring out a certain episode in his late life in 1469, when he was already more than seventy years old. After the death of his brother, Toscanelli had to pick up the family fortunes and to steer the family firm through the adventures of the Gold Rush of Florence; by which I mean the alum strike in the Tolfa hills which changed so many fortunes around. He did it very successfully. This is the kind of thing that would make a Marxist happy. Garin is far too subtle to let himself be drawn into a trap of that kind: he goes on to characterize his subject in his more old-fashioned interests—but there is no denying that he enjoys setting up Toscanelli's likes, the technicians, against the orators who have adorned and also afflicted Italian culture in the centuries from then till now.

Let us look at Toscanelli, then, first by way of his Florentine friends.

The chief character in that group is, no doubt, Filippo Brunelleschi, the master who brought forth Renaissance architecture. Both as artist and as technologist I have to take him for granted. I should like simply to present him as an innovator, and a radical innovator at that.

With him, as I have tried to show elsewhere, we have for the first time the master engineer of a new type backed by the prestige of mathematics and the "recondite secrets of perspective." (Galileo's slightly tongue-in-cheek description of his own achievements with the telescope is certainly valid here because the man *is* the inventor of perspective.) Brunelleschi is a man whose capacity is not supposed to have been due to long experience and trade secrets but to strength of intellect and theoretical boldness; a man who can speak his mind in the councils of the city and is granted patents for his engineering devices. His judges are no small people either, if you come to think of the group of regents that then ran the cathedral works. The regents and their advisers are men like Niccolò da Uzzano, Niccolò Niccoli, Poggio, Traversari, Palla Strozzi, and, not least, the young Cosimo de' Medici. Men of affairs, most of them, wearers of the "lucco," the red cape of the Council of the Republic, humanists and statesmen all, involved in the European issues of their day, sponsors of the unification of the eastern and western churches, hosts of the last true ecumenic council, when Pope and Patriarch of Byzantium and their retinues, assembled within its walls, made Florence for the time the capital of Christendom.

Certainly we have here, then, something which is reaching world dimensions in general acknowledgment, and new types of men are arising. Donatello may be acquainted with the Latin classics while Brunelleschi is not; but still, it is Brunelleschi who stands as a qualified intellectual of a new type. It is only a century later that the fateful distinction emerges between pure and applied art. By that time the pure artist himself is hardly an intellectual.

Finally, this complex of achievements by a well-known group of great talents—Manetti, Ghiberti, Donatello, Masaccio, Uccello, Luca della Robbia, with Brunelleschi as leader—found a literary expounder of comparable talent in the person of Leone Battista Alberti to give their ideas full citizenship in the robed world of letters and humanism, something that only Galileo was able later to achieve by himself. It will have been a fragile and fleeting conjunction, no doubt; it will end up in mere academicism, and in theories about art, and just about the time when science breaks forth with its own ideas of method and truth; but as long as it lasts, in the period of creation, it is a true conjunction, two in one. Leon Battista Alberti only paraphrases Filippo's words—we know that—when he says of the new art of architecture, "If it ever was written in the past, we have dug it up, and if it was not, we have drawn it from heaven." (This is a very typical, concisely expressed Renaissance position that leaves both possibilities open.) That "social breakthrough" of the new science of Galileo effected through the telescope, we find here in an early counterpart or rather in its first rehearsal. Everyone in 1450 was aware that a boldly speculative theory had preceded the complex of achievements, until the "cupolone," the great dome of the cathedral, rose unsupported in its greatness; "ample enough," says Alberti, "to hold in its shade all the land of Tuscany."

So there is in Toscanelli's time the feeling of revolution. I have tried elsewhere to characterize such a feeling phenomenologically: it is the resolute assumption of responsibility that forms the criterion. And that is why, in the moment of the Galilean crisis, we know there is a revolution because Galileo assumes the responsibility, in the face of the doctrine of the Church, to consider himself the only authority, or, if you like, the most authorized consultant, in a matter in which that authority has not been formally assigned to him.

To return to our present task: we are trying to define one of those rare points where art and science undeniably join. Brunelleschi created his theory of perspective by experimental means. He built the earliest optical instrument after the eyeglasses, the last one before the telescope—his famous perspective tablet. It had the new element of measurement in it, and it presupposed the establishment of a system of co-ordinates. To quote Krautheimer: "Plans and elevation drawn to scale were fundamental innovations in architectural tooling that he was the first to introduce in Florence." Seen from our point of view, these remarks of the historian of art seem an almost bizarre understatement. The introduction of measurement in its proper place in a theoretical treatment of reality is an innovation in intellectual tooling which is probably the most decisive factor of the scientific revolution. It advances step by step into our own time, and its originality has to be traced in the early stages.

The vibrating strings of the Pythagoreans, the angular measurements of the astronomers, the measurements that transfer the study of aesthetic proportion to projective techniques—all are stages that we should work back into. And after that, of course, the way was open for the adventures through the theory of light and for the camera obscura. Here, implicitly, a new theory of space is born and a new geometrization of space and light, the new conception of central perspective which places man in an isotropic, in non-Aristotelian, space. Anyone who has been to visit casually the Pazzi Chapel in Santa Croce in Florence, which is Brunelleschi's most typical work, after having been in a Gothic cathedral, knows that he is facing an entirely different world of space and that the escape in some symbolic direction is denied to him; he is inside central perspective. And Copernicus is, in a way, the one who brings true central perspective to the universe, by placing "the lamp of the universe in the center." All of this implies, indicates, or in various ways announces the moving of the study of reality from imaginary or symbolic into real space.

And now we come to Master Paul the physician. Born in 1397, Paolo dal Pozzo Toscanelli was Brunelleschi's junior by twenty years. He came of a family of rich merchants. Their house was near what is now Palazzo Pitti, on the other side of the Arno. There is a tablet to mark its site. We even have the census that was taken in 1400 of their estate. The Toscanelli family was described as having in town nineteen servants, two horses, and a mule: the three-car garage, so to speak. In other words, they were rich and influential Florentine businessmen.

From his childhood, young Paolo knew Brunelleschi. As soon as he came back (in 1425) from Padua, where he had been studying for the doctorate, he and Brunelleschi were guests at a dinner in the garden of a friend, where they sealed their friendship; and thereafter they became inseparable for the next thirty years. As Toscanelli used to say later when he was an old man, "This was the greatest association of my life." He added, "You should try to understand what Brunelleschi has done because what he did takes great intentness of mind, more knowledge than you think, and also great circumspection." These words are quite significant of both men. Brunelleschi—or Maestro Pippo, as they called him—was (like Leonardo) a "man without letters," that is, he did not know Latin. In fact, his only books seem to have been Dante and the Bible. But he was a scientific and engineering genius, and he readily absorbed the geometry that Toscanelli gave him. Toscanelli had to be sent to Padua to study medicine; he came back with the title of Doctor of Medicine and was generally called "the physician." Actually, the curriculum included mathematics. You may notice that Copernicus went down to Italy and got the title of Doctor of Medicine. And in fact, if Toscanelli stands in the background as a medical man, a cartographer, an astrologer, he is essentially a mathematician; and one of such considerable achievements that the great expert of the time, Regiomontanus, in writing to him calls him a "second Archimedes." This is, of course, a rhetorical or humanistic compliment because neither writer nor recipient can be considered in the line of work of Archimedes, but it is a set way of expressing admiration.

It was a wonderful conjunction, that of the architect and the geometrician, so early in the century, planning together the first great feat of modern engineering, the cupola of the cathedral rising unsupported on its base without scaffoldings or centerings toward the sky. And in the lantern of the cathedral, once it was built, Brunelleschi had an aperture made for his friend to project a beam of light down on a sundial on the floor of the cathedral. It was the greatest sundial in the world, then, because the beam was 240 feet long. On that sundial, on that "gnomon" as they called it, Toscanelli measured again with great precision the precession of the equinoxes and the inclination of the ecliptic so as to consecrate, so to speak, the double value of the cathedral.

In those years lies the beginning.

If one were to assign a high point to the Renaissance, one might suggest just those years—the decade, say, between 1428 and 1438, which began with the state visit of Prince Pedro of Portugal to Florence, where he was received with unsurpassed magnificence and a spectacular procession but also was given all the maps and geographical material that he had been asking for, and ended on the ecumenic council which brought together for the last time eastern and western Christendom and insured the passage of Greece into Europe.

It is not without significance that Melanchthon, the representative of the new culture, was to say of Florence a century later, and in carefully measured words, that it was for him the center of world learning. For after all, in a world in which philosophy and theology held such a high place, Paris or even Oxford might have preserved valid claims for the rank. And Florence was not even a university town. It might have been chided as intellectually irregular. Yet it is the center which not only brought to Europe the high and subtle speculations of Neoplatonism but also the texts of Archimedes; it brought forth venture capitalism, and with it a new class of technicians who went ahead in a most venturesome way. It is they who discovered America by mistake, gave it its name by another mistake, built the new cupola, as scholars insisted bitterly, by guess and by God, or as humanists said, "with their false and lying geometry," tried Leonardo's machines, and with the new geometry of space opened the way for that other mad venture whose author was to get at last his richly deserved comeuppance —I mean Galileo himself. If we think of the rigor and prudence of the Paris doctors, we must agree that this is a different view of intellectual leadership.

To return to Toscanelli and the geometrization of space, we should not forget that if in youth he was the junior adviser of Brunelleschi, he became later the senior guide, philosopher, and friend of many, including the great theoretician of perspective, Leon Battista Alberti, the man for whom was coined the title of *uomo universale*. Of them all, Toscanelli was the only one with a real scientific training. He was something, if I may say so, of a quiet Kepler—if a quiet Kepler can be imagined—and it is only when one thinks of it that one is grateful for Kepler's engaging and irrepressible gift of gab.

It is to Toscanelli that Alberti dedicated his dialogues, the *Intercænales*, or *Table Talks*, those witty conversations which came into so many hands and were to be a model for Erasmus. A singular choice: it is not the treatise on perspective he offers him, but a commentary on society. "As you are a doctor of bodies," wrote Alberti, "so I am trying to be a doctor of souls." The hazy figure of the master is outlined here in the direction of worldly wisdom and knowledge of men, as befits a doctor.

So far we remain within the cultural circle of Florence. But now we have to go far afield.

One of the most commanding figures of the fifteenth century is Nicholas of Cusa, or Cusanus, or the Cardinal of Cusa, the great German prelate. His influence was immense in northern Europe. It sparked the thought of men like Copernicus and

Kepler, and, not least, Bruno, for he was the first one to suggest responsibly the infinity of the universe and the mobility—at least some kind of mobility—of the earth. One wonders about this man finding himself such an Italianate German and yet such a misfit at the Court of Rome where he was actually prime minister. One wonders what Aeneas Sylvius, the elegant and worldly man of letters who reigned over the golden age of humanism as Pope Pius II, must have thought of his friend's involved speculations. He may have decided that Nicholas was too good an administrator and diplomat to be wasted on such subtleties, but it apparently enhanced his authority to philosophize thus paradoxically in the obscure manner of the "ultramontanes."

There is no doubt that with Nicholas, German philosophy has entered the scene full-fledged, with some of its powerful characteristics well in evidence, and he makes one think very much of that future continuator of his work, Gottfried Wilhelm Leibniz.

The central fact about Cusanus, which has been too often overlooked because he scored no achievements in science proper, is that he is an imaginative mathematical temperament who has taken up in the raw stage the modern idea of mathematics as a "science of the infinite." This idea, in itself, undercuts radically the conventional and rather simple-minded notion, entertained by the scholastics, of mathematics as the science of magnitude, that is, "of the more and the less." He does not deal simply with irrelevant sizes; he deals with the essence of things, because at the core of things there is understood to be the infinite. If mathematics is the science of the infinite—and this is indeed what the great Greek mathematicians had discovered in their own way and what Aristotle had tried to cover up—why, then, one's metaphysical emotions are apt to respond. To a mind with a medieval training, infinity participates in the divine essence, and should be understood to be somehow at the core of all things. Mathematics ceases to be a science of mere abstractions and becomes a possible avenue to a true knowledge of reality. Yet there is one side to these speculations which strikes any scientific reader as helpless. Anyone, indeed, who reads Cusanus critically will get the curious impression of an inadequately fused intellectual enterprise. There is, no doubt, a creative intuition in the play with mathematical concepts; then there appear new, technically advanced ideas which are not followed up but left to die on the vine. The developments about the relative position and the mobility of the earth around its orbit are one instance. It is as if Cusanus were led on by a thought that he has not fully mastered. We experience such "double takes" in reading Plato, too, but then we know that he was trying to adjust into his speculations the advanced work of contemporary mathematicians like Eudoxus which he had not fully grasped either.

Now who is there back of Cusanus? Philosophers have answered a little too easily by saying the Pythagorean tradition. Surely. It is back of everything and very clearly at the back of such a man. But there is nowhere in Pythagorean tradition this idea of mathematics as the science of the infinite, nor are there those technical developments about relativistic geometry. This is what philosophers have overlooked, and this is also where the historians of science may help.

For Nicholas had one bosom friend of his student days and later, one with whom he had "thought together" during the formative years in Padua, to whom he was to dedicate more than one of his works and in particular his artless little treatise on the squaring of the circle—and that friend was Toscanelli.

It was still Toscanelli who, when his friend Nicholas lay dying a lonely death on the road in the little town of Todi, almost two hundred miles away, hurried to his bedside, at sixty-seven years of age, to share the last vigils.

So those curious seeds of a new mathematical thought, which the cardinal seized upon with his powerful imagination but could not develop adequately, may well have come from Toscanelli himself. From whom else? There was no one else around. And, in fact, there are some significant confirmations.

If the historians of thought have not seen it hitherto, it is because they misread both men. Because the cardinal's mathematics was dismissed disdainfully by Regiomontanus as insignificant—which is a technically correct judgment—they did not see that the man's imagination was that of a creative analyst in the modern sense.

On the other hand, because Toscanelli is etched in history primarily as a doctor of medicine and a practical consultant in so many fields from applied geometry to cartography because he is kept in the background, because his advice was asked in the matter of buildings and crops and maps and horoscopes and financial computations, because he did not participate in the lofty metaphysics and the luminous transcendental vaporings of Marsilio Ficino nor in the orotund declamations and the golden Platonic eloquence of the Florentine academy; he has been adjudged a modest technician and, at best, an outstanding medical man. And it is very true that Toscanelli gave out results and kept his thoughts to himself, as contemporaries witness. In fact, he wrote nothing at all beyond letters. And those letters are lost—all except the one that Columbus got hold of. But it is quite a letter, as is well known.

And so it was forgotten that he was also a thinker of strange thoughts.

Those thoughts could not very well be grasped by Ficino, the official philosopher, for all that he wrote of Paolo with high praise and indeed adulation. They were very special thoughts. We shall deal with them in a moment. I am trying to see from many angles this constellation of minds which really gives rise to the intellectual Renaissance from Florence to Germany.

There is one feature which has made Toscanelli famous; and although this particular fame is not wholly deserved, it will serve to make up for what he has missed otherwise. I speak of his letter to Portugal concerning the chances of a discovery of a new world.

Here again, we come into one of those high points of a cultural life in which everything seems to tie up with everything, in which the mobile tissue of time becomes almost tangible.

In the year 1474, Marsilio Ficino wrote to Bandini that he had concluded his great book on Platonic theology—which was to come out only later, in 1482, the year of Toscanelli's death. On the twenty-fifth of June of that same year, 1474, at the height of the reign of Lorenzo il Magnifico, in the slightly corrupt splendor of that court which was shooting its last sparklers, Paolo Toscanelli, or Paul the physician as he usually signed, wrote a letter to a Portuguese ecclesiastic called Fernam Martins concerning the possibility of a route to the East by way of the West and joined with it a map he had constructed of the possible route. This Canon Fernam Martins, the recipient of the letter, he had met ten years previously at the bedside of the dying Cardinal of Cusa in Todi. Thus fate works in strange ways.

We have the letter as it was transcribed by Columbus himself on the flyleaf of a book. So he must have given it deep consideration. Was it the first cause of his enterprise? Was the underestimated distance of Asia, derived from Strabo's wrong data, an incentive to his voyage? Italian scholars, proud of having this Genoese navigator guided by a Florentine cosmographer, have made a great to-do about it. I myself doubt that it was as decisive as often suggested. Philologists think in terms of classical authors, but technicians have their own sources of information. Columbus had quite reliable maps really—not on the Spanish side, of course: he had that of Fra Mauro of Venice, he had the Genoese map of 1457, the Catalan map of 1375—and they all gave the correct distances within about 10 per cent; so I take it he knew what he was doing. He knew, then, what an adventure it was to set out on a voyage on an unbroken ocean— except for a chain of islands, he hoped—which would take him from Spain to China.

But there is more in a culture than is inscribed in its rational decisions. If Toscanelli acted on Columbus, it was because, as a recognized expert in the stars, he gave him a sense of the urgency of fate. This is the true tension of the Renaissance: this context of political in-fighting and prophetic vision, of heroic vocations and cunning cynicism, of magic, astrology, prophecy, and great new scientific ideas all in one.

In the margin of his own copy of Pierre D'Ailly, Columbus transcribes the lines of Scripture: "The heavens proclaim the glory of God." He is haunted by the power of the cosmos and by a sense of his own calling. Columbus is a man who is quite well inside his own culture; and when he combines Pliny and

Pierre D'Ailly and Albumasar, he does exactly what an educated man of his time would have done. For right at the time when Pico della Mirandola wrote so passionately and rationally against astrology and protested against the camouflaging of the Virgin Mary as a constellation, Columbus was transcribing with his own hand a famous text of the Arab astronomer Albumasar: "There ascends in the first aspect a virgin holding two ears of wheat in her hand . . . and she holds a child to her heart."

The great prophetic theme of the return of Virgo, which inspires Virgil's Fourth Eclogue and is echoed through the Middle Ages, reappears here in full force. But how transformed. Witness the Latin lines of John of Garland in his *Stella Maris*:

> Ut Albumasar testatur
> Inter stellas declaratur
> Virgo lactans puerum.

"As Albumasar witnesseth, a virgin is declared among the stars, nursing a child to her heart."

It is a most considerable mix-up.

Albumasar, around this time, had become a name to conjure with. The first printed editions of his *Introductorium* and of his *Great Conjunctions* were not to come out until 1489, but there were enough manuscript copies around to spread alarm and despondency in Florence already in 1460, and the talk was all of comets and cataclysms. Albumasar, as they called him, or rather Abu Mashar, for that was his name, was an Arab astrologer who died in 886. He is not accounted technically an astronomer. He shines indeed as an astronomer so little that my friend Willy Hartner, the immensely scholarly and rigorous historian of astronomy, dismisses him as a vapid chatterer and

wonders how Tycho Brahe himself could have quoted him at
the side of Al Battani. The answer, I dare say, lies right in
Hartner's paper which traces this unknown reference. Why did
people mention him? Tycho was a great technician of astronomy, but he was also a Renaissance man. So, once he had made,
by measuring parallaxes, his epoch-making discovery that comets
and novae are in outer space, he thought nothing of quoting
Abu Mashar for a confirmation, although the man had no concern with parallaxes. This is not the only time that astrology
has lent a helping hand to science. Up to the time of Kepler,
astronomy and astrology are so closely intermingled that a man's
thought moves freely between them. Allow me to remind you
in my turn of that *locus classicus* in *Troilus and Cressida*.

And so here we come to another crucial case. Those lines I
have quoted of John of Garland in his *Stella Maris* are part of
the new Christian enterprise to refer all constellation properties
to the Virgin Mary seen as Virgo, in other words to build up a
spiritual astrology inside orthodoxy. And this in turn is due to
Abu Mashar, who had announced the exaltation of the Virgin
with Child in the heavens. This could not but strike a deep
chord in the hearts of a civilization which still believed in Virgil
as the prophet of the advent of Christ—the prophet of the
Gentiles:

Incipe, parve puer, cui non risere parentes.[1]

That a Moslem should come now bringing Virgil's *nova
progenies* explicitly as a child suckling at Virgo's breast is surely
one of the more amusing cross-purposes of history. It could
have provided a good finale for Comparetti's classic work on
Virgil in the Middle Ages.

But in truth, the infidel still managed to serve the purposes of infidelity. We should see what he was saying. He is not really announcing, like Virgil, the return of Virgo, or Justice, to earth. This had happened about Anno Domini, with other great signs in heaven: Virgo had come to one of the four crucial points of the ecliptic, the vernal equinox. This was "earth" in the traditional archaic language. The next "return" would be when she reached a solstitial point, a further quarter-turn of the precession, another four thousand years away from us. Rather, Abu Mashar was speaking of Venus coming to a particular aspect in Virgo; and he was using the Oriental symbolism of portraying Venus in this position (for it was Venus who was the protagonist) as a mother with child. This came straight from Babylon: "Inanna with the child in her lap," as the Babylonian hymn puts it; and Inanna is a name for Ishtar. In another symmetrical position, close to Sirius, she was Ishtar the Harlot, *Venus Pandemia*, an abandoned woman. There are some comic repercussions to this so remote theme. Father Kugler, the great historian of Babylonian astronomy who wrote a generation ago, still could not countenance the sea-change of the Lady Ishtar into a woman of loose conduct. It was contrary, he said, to the avowed respect of the Babylonians for moral principles and motherhood to have their chief female deity first impersonate the divine mother with child and then a trot. He suggested the protagonist of this transformation scene must be Sirius the Dog, so essentially associated with Venus in the Sothic cycle, which is marked by their joint heliacal rising. Alas, Fr. Kugler let himself be carried away by his moral fervor. Venus is standing in her own right in both positions.

These things still hurt, apparently: the great feminine principle seen as both mother and demon, the devil himself, the

"Frau Venus" of *Tannhäuser*. This it was that came with the expounding of the doctrine by those who knew: dreadful ambiguity in heaven itself, Venus dominant under the cloak of Virgo. This it was that the interpreters of heaven were explaining quietly to some, denying to others. Not the least of the tensions of that strange fifteenth century is laid between the two poles of Venus Anadyomene rising from the sea and the Virgin worshiped in ascetic meditation.

Without those tensions, how could we understand the Church desperately trying to Christianize astrology and hugging this asp to her breast? How could we understand the furious and apocalyptic reaction of Savonarola, the sacking and the burning, Botticelli abandoning his pagan imagery for prayer, Pico della Mirandola forsaking his learning, his esoteric knowledge, his wonderful idea of man in the cockpit of the universe, to attack astrology and end his life in passionate renouncement?

The doctrines of Fate and Freedom were strong drinks to be mixed for an age of transition. Think of Leonardo's great series of drawings of the end of the world in storms of wind and fire, of Columbus' memory of Blessed Joachim of Fiora. Toscanelli, the "cosmographer," as they called him, is doing his part in a wise and statesmanlike way. He refused the astrology of nativities and death signs—we have his own statements on that—but concentrated on cycles of change and renewal, and quietly announced the imminent discovery of a new world. He defines, in a way, the Renaissance itself, in what it has of nascent and renascent. In his letter to Martins, he dreams of wonderful distant cities and unknown civilizations in the spirit of Sir Thomas More. He imagines rivers in that new world with as many as two hundred cities along their banks. But unlike Sir Thomas More, he is writing before, not after, the event. With

his authority he is now telling Columbus that something unprecedented is bound to happen—he is giving him a sense of
impending fate.

I trust I will not be misunderstood. The historian of science
must see what is living and operating at a given time, in order
to find the true context of ideas. The main context of the
Renaissance is the changing idea of the cosmos, but a cosmos
first and last it had to be; and what is there that holds the key
to the comos except astrology? It stays in that key position until
it is replaced by celestial mechanics—and replaced only in a
manner of speaking, for the cosmos does not last long without
it. Descartes is in the offing. Astrology, then, dominated medicine
and physics as the most comprehensive science. Notice the
curious relationship you find in Ficino's work; Ficino is officially
against astrology, as was his pupil Pico—but he cannot help
believing in it all the same. Ficino cannot ignore astrology for
the simple reason that Neoplatonism cannot do without it; and
Plato himself, the late Plato of astro-theology, had been leading
great philosophies back to the Babylonian cocoon. So it is very
hard to imagine Ficino not able to believe in astrology, Pico
himself not able to believe in astrology. Although Pico attacked
it violently, he attacked it as an ambiguous dangerous presence,
not as a vain pseudoscience. Astrology tied up heaven and earth
in one system, which led men to search for regularities, for the
laws of periodicity and change. He who thinks that there is
only trash in the books of Albumasar, of Guido Bonatti, of
Cardan, of Abu Ezra, of Pietro d'Abano, of al-Kalisi or Cecco
d'Ascoli—or, may I add, in the writings of Father Athanasius
Kircher himself, although he lived in quite another century—is
in for a surprise. Those men were among the first minds of their
times. They certainly had more to say than many humanistic

philosophers, so called. They were philosophers in the key of a great *techne*, as the Greek would have said, fully formed specialists. In their work we find documents of half-lost religions, remarkable fragments of psychology of the unconscious, important data of geography—for one had to relate exactly places to celestial time—as well as ideas about physiology, about historical cycles, about the character of nations and men, and, of course, some of the best professional astronomy of the time. Kepler is their last offshoot.

It would be well if we could know more about Cecco d'Ascoli. The God-fearing souls have shied away from him because he was burned by the Inquisition, the rationalists have forgotten about him because he believed in astrology. The misunderstanding goes on. We have lost the key to those poems of his which are true cryptograms, and they are certainly not devoid of some important meaning. He did not like Dante; and it cannot be for the reason that he alleges—that Dante was a "man of little faith." But he must have had a singular faith of his own, and a strong one, if it allowed him to face the stake, like Giordano Bruno, instead of submitting. We may get a hint of it in his scornful lines:

> Qui non si canta al modo del poeta
> Che finge immaginando cose vane
> Ma qui resplende e luce onne natura
> Che a chi entende fa la mente leta.

"Here we do not sing after the manner of the poet, who invents, imagining vain things, but here shines in dazzling light every nature [i.e., essence] which fills with joy him who understands."

There could be no clearer statement of the dichotomy between the two cultures—except in certain bitter remarks of Leonardo. What is attacked here, as early as 1325, is not so much the past as what is coming, the literary humanism of the Renaissance, man divorced from the cosmos.

And this in turn should finally give the clue to Toscanelli's philosophical personality. Modern critics have ignored or minimized many remarkable things that were said insistently about him with great respect and veneration—that he was pious and ascetic, that he kept strict chastity and abstained from eating meat. They thought this too goody-goody. They were wrong. For these traits prove Toscanelli to have been a true Pythagorean of the old observance—not simply one of those romantics fascinated by the magic of number, but one in whom there lived again the thought and behavior of the ancient sect. Landino called him "a venerable image of antiquity." He is indeed an original Pythagorean in his strange combination of mathematics, inductive research, practical interests, and a worship of the colossal machinery of cosmic cycles. Where did he get his data? From Arab astronomy, from lost sources, by word of mouth. There is such a knowledge that scholars a little too deliberately ignore. It is seeded here and there by what I have once called the "Jetstream of Time." When we find similar behavior in Leonardo da Vinci—including the vegetarian obsession—and strange bits of information about ancient traditions which are in no text but reappear at odd points in the Renaissance, notably in Jerome Cardan, we have at least some clue as to where they came from.

Men who had those ideas were careful, as was Toscanelli himself, who never talked about his theories. What he gave to the public were results. The only piece of his own that we have is his computation of the comet of 1460. It is an excellent computation, as Celoria has shown, and agrees with the figures of Regiomontanus quite perfectly. Above is written in a shaky hand—probably his, and these are the only words we have in his own hand—"The immense labors and grievous vigils of Paolo Toscanelli on the measurement of the comet." ("Immensi labores et graves vigiliae Pauli de Puteo Toscanelli super mensuram comete.") That is all. It is like an invocation. The measure was the thing. These measures in heaven were for him the important cesuras of the universe, and who should contradict him on that? Professor Bush has quoted Brandes' remark that Voltaire respected very few things in heaven and earth but he respected the uniform caesura. Well, we all love Voltaire—at least, I love Voltaire—but his tragedies are terrible, and you cannot say that the uniform caesura saved him. The master astrologer's caesuras might have still more meaning.

Allow me to think it significant that a man who sparked so many new ideas in his own time should be the one in whom the most ancient frame of ideas had been reborn: that the new scientific thought should have as its precondition the rebirth of a cosmology going back to the gray dawn of antiquity. It is only now that we are beginning to form an idea of the scope and size of the cosmology that was shaped between 5000 and 2000 B.C. and was inherited only in fragments by historic civilizations as we know them. It is hard to imagine the immense intellectual effort it entailed, hard to measure its philosophical scope, which is clothed in myth and only symbolically, technically expressed in its planetary and precessional cycles. It is a lost world coming gradually into view, like a lost continent emerging from the ocean. But Plato still knew about it, at least parts of it, if we are to understand something of his clear technical implications.

Nor is Toscanelli the last to have searched for it, for after him comes Johann Kepler, his most legitimate successor and, like him, a passionate defender of astrology, although he was a Copernican. Let me conclude, then, with some words of Kepler that Toscanelli would have signed gladly himself: "The ways in which men came into the knowledge of things celestial appears to me almost as marvelous as the nature of those things itself." As Brunelleschi had started out as the earliest archeologist—for that is what he did in his twenties when he and Donatello went to Rome and started digging like men possessed: the Romans thought they were looking for treasures, but they were digging in the ruins of Rome for the secrets of the ancient architects—so Toscanelli had revived remote doctrines of cosmology and found there his inspiration. Nascent or renascent, let us remember Alberti's words: "If they were written, we have dug them up, and if they were not, we have snatched them from heaven."

In the search for the hidden sources of ancient knowledge, for the meaning of "prophetic language," even Isaac Newton himself was to spend the latter half of his life. Who are we, then, to assess casually the "immense labors and the grievous vigils" of the man whom the Florentines called Maestro Pagolo, or Paul the physician?

---

1. Or maybe Norden is right in reading "qui non risere parenti," the child has not yet laughed to its mother, a great theme in cosmological tradition.

MUSIC OF THE RENAISSANCE
AS VIEWED BY RENAISSANCE MUSICIANS

By

Edward E. Lowinsky

THE QUESTION OF TRADITION AND INNOVATION in the Renaissance has exercised a great many minds in the last several decades. The views differ in different fields. They differ even in the same field. In the words of Erwin Panofsky, "During the last forty or fifty years the 'Renaissance problem' has become one of the most hotly debated issues in modern historiography."[1]

It is this state of affairs which laid the accent, in this volume, on the conception that the man of the Renaissance had of himself and of his civilization. This should provide us with a valuable corrective of whatever views we hold of the epoch. The self-appraisal of an epoch forms an integral part of its historical essence. It is not all the evidence, but it is so significant a part of it that we cannot afford to neglect it if we are to arrive at a balanced view of its character.

In speaking of the views of the musicians writing in the fifteenth and sixteenth centuries, we use the term "musician" as referring, in the first place, to writers on music. However,

whereas many prominent medieval theorists were mathematicians, most Renaissance writers concerned with music were
practical musicians. Tinctoris, Gafori, Aron, Coclico, Vicentino,
Zarlino were composers and singers or choirmasters as well as
theorists of music.

What a change of scenery in the field of Renaissance literature
on music as against the Middle Ages: the stage moves from
the quiet monastic cell, in which most medieval works on music
were conceived, to the noisy places of musical performance, the
choirloft, the rehearsal rooms of town musicians, the house of
the boy choristers, the humanistic gymnasium, the private concert halls of nobles and patricians. For these are the places in
which the new writers on music, whether they be churchmen
or laymen, are working. Choirmasters and composers, singers
and instrumentalists, acousticians and connoisseurs, school teachers, humanists, and that new breed of men who were not players
or singers or composers but who judged the art and skill of all
of them, the critics—they all were now beginning to write about
music. The printing presses of Naples, Venice, Milan, Bologna,
Rome, Lyons, Paris, Leipzig, Nuremberg, Augsburg, Witten-
berg, and Basel were kept busy by their industrious pens.

The gulf between theory and practice, painfully obvious in
medieval theory, was closed in Renaissance writings on music.
At no time, before or later, was there more intimate contact
between theorists, composers, performers, connoisseurs, critics,
and the public than in the hundred years between Tinctoris and
Vincenzo Galilei, spokesman for the Florentine Camerata—one
hundred years that mark the high tide of the musical thought
of the Renaissance. Galilei, humanistically inspired,[2] introduced
—and Monteverdi codified—a split between "old" counterpoint
obeying a complex system of rules and "modern" music, affect-

oriented and striving for monodic dominance of the poetic word, between *prima* and *seconda prattica.* This resulted in a split in baroque theory between a "forward" and a "backward" look, which the theory of music has not overcome since.

In comparing medieval views on music with those of the Renaissance, we must not commit the error of treating medieval theory as one static body of unchanging views. For one thing, the new spirit of criticism and experimental science in the thirteenth and fourteenth centuries, the recovery of Aristotle, the contact with Arab civilization, and the rise of the universities could not fail to make their impact on the arts and the theory of the arts.[3] For another, the medieval theorists, many of whom were mathematicians—music having been assigned to the mathematical disciplines of the quadrivium—were trying constantly to keep their theories, rooted as they were in mathematical tradition, in touch with the musical reality of their days. Minstrels and folk singers, jongleurs and instrumentalists, who gained favor in high and low circles alike, knew nothing of their theories and cared less, neither did their audience. Composers of polyphonic art music, on the other hand, had to break away from a system restricting the use of consonances to fourths, fifths, and octaves. The task of the medieval theorist, therefore, was one of constant accommodation between Pythagorean dogma and musical reality. It could not fail that in this process one group of theorists would incline toward mathematical dogmatism, another toward musical reality; and this picture was complicated by the various positions taken toward the constant flux of new developments in the polyphonic art music. It is this unceasing, stubborn, yet fruitful, tug of war which was pushing slowly but surely toward a frontier where new problems arose that could not be solved any longer in the framework of medieval attitudes, an evolution which proceeded in a constant up and down of advance, reaction, and new advance.

The historian's purpose must be threefold: to define the character of the new, to do justice to its embryonic development, and to fix the date of its birth. The theme of this volume favors the first and the last objectives, but we shall suggest, at least in occasional side glances, the existence of evolutionary trends of Renaissance attitudes within the matrix of medieval thought.

The frequent union of practical musician and theorist in one and the same artist gives the Renaissance writers on music a special authority on the questions we wish to ask of them. Do they themselves recognize the existence of a "renaissance in music," a conscious departure from the past, an intended revival and restoration of the art, an inspiration in ideas of antiquity, a discovery of new means of musical organization brought about by a new aesthetics, a new philosophy of music? An attempt at presenting the contemporary evidence faithfully and impartially means to present conflicting evidence. For the Renaissance writers on music speak not with one voice but in a polyphony of voices not devoid of dissonance and discord.

THE CLASH OF OLD AND NEW

Did the musicians, the writers on music, and the aestheticians of the epoch consider the music of their time as new? This is the first question to which we need an answer.

In a famous passage of his work *De arte contrapuncti*, written in 1477, the Flemish theorist of music, Johannes Tinctoris, who lived for the greatest part of his life at the court of Naples as singer, composer, teacher, and writer, said: "Although it seems beyond belief, there does not exist a single piece of music, not composed within the last forty years, that is regarded by the learned as worth hearing."[4] In other words, Tinctoris, writing in 1477, dates the beginning of "modern" music from 1437 or, say, roughly, 1435. As leaders of the new generation of composers, he mentions Ockeghem and Busnois; he singles out their teachers, the Englishman Dunstable and the two composers of the Burgundian era, Binchois and Dufay.

Tinctoris states this view also in his treatise on proportions. There he speaks of the music of his day as an *ars nova* and sketches the background of this new art in these words: "The fountain and origin of this new art lies with the English, whose leading master was Dunstable. His French contemporaries were Dufay and Binchois who were immediately succeeded by the moderns"—*moderni*[5] is the word used by Tinctoris—"Ockeghem, Busnois, Regis, and Caron, who of all those whom I have heard are the most outstanding in composition."[6]

Comparing the Franco-Netherlanders with the English of his day, Tinctoris gives his preference to the former, observing that "they freshly create new works day by day, whereas the English—and this is a sign of a terrible lack of talent—use one and the same style of composition."[7]

For us today, novelty, originality, individuality have become unquestioned criteria in judging intellectual and artistic achievement; indeed, in some cases they may have become a fetish of contemporary art. In Tinctoris' day, these criteria were by no means generally accepted. The medieval view of the divine origin, and hence of the artistic perfection, of the Gregorian chant still had eloquent protagonists in the Renaissance. The most prominent of these was Johannes Gallicus, a Carthusian monk and important writer on music, who died in 1473, and whose education is summarized best in his own words: "France bore me and made me a singer. Italy, however, under Vittorino da Feltre, a man imbued with Greek as well as Latin letters, made me a musician and grammarian, such as I am."[8]

Here is what Gallicus says on the Gregorian chant: "Who, I pray, would not know that no mention of Plain Chant exists before the advent of our Saviour, and that this angelic and solemn style of singing was given to us Christians more by the Holy Spirit than by humans?"[9] The belief in the divine perfection of an art must needs lead to a belief in one single, immutable art form and to opposition against any new form of art. This view was held widely in the Middle Ages. It was still shared by Johannes Gallicus, who inveighed against the new polyphony that brought about a new art of mensural notation with an infinity of new notes, signs, ligatures, and the like. The new art that filled Tinctoris with admiration causes Johannes Gallicus to erupt in a veritable philippic: "In various cyphers and diverse signs and characters they frivolously perform all day long new and vain songs crazily devising stupid inventions in their proportions which they do not understand. Indeed, those familiar with these so-called mensural compositions often fill them with cyphers and novel fancies so that even their own creators have trouble in performing them; nevertheless they praise them, glorying in so vile an enterprise as if they had achieved a great thing. What good, o singers, is this your madness! Shall this noble science of ours be subjected to your cyphers? Far be it! Sing, I pray, sing! Break your tones[10] as you please, think out daily new sweet and tintillating songs, waste your time on longs, breves, semibreves, minims! And even though you knew all this perfectly, but nothing else, I should not call you true singers, let alone musicians."[11]

The sharp divergence of views as to the value of what Tinctoris calls "ars nova" and Gallicus "novae phantasiae" is based on a radical disagreement concerning the function of music. Gallicus upbraids the singers of his day for taking more pleasure in singing for the people than for God, for letting their vanity, as he says, "seduce, bind, inebriate them with their frivolous songs, for talent goes where the mind directs it. But no one has served well two masters, as God himself has testified."[12]

Although disciple of a humanist, albeit a "Christian humanist" (Vittorino da Feltre), Gallicus, the Carthusian monk, espouses the extreme view of medieval orthodoxy that might be paraphrased in the words: "musica ancilla theologiae." If it is music's single function to please God, and if God through the Holy Ghost has inspired Pope Gregory to write down the divine chant, the *cantus angelicus,* as Gallicus calls it, then the musician's function is limited to the performance of the chant, and all writing of new compositions (with the whole intricate enterprise of mensural music) is nothing but frivolity, the more so since, with its many notes in many voices, it obscures rather than illuminates the sacred word. When Gallicus speaks of restoration, he means, in theory, a return to Boethius; in practice, a return to the pristine simplicity of the chant,[13] although he disclaims any intent to deal with theory as such except when necessary. When he finds that the *patres antiqui* did not use more than fifteen notes, he rejects the attempts to expand the range of the tone system in these words: "But such frivolity did not please Father Gregory."[14]

In the center of Tinctoris' manifold writings on music stands, solidly fixed, "Man."[15] This is why secular and liturgical music mingle in his treatises in easy and equal companionship; this is why, in all musical questions, the ear and artistic judgment reign supreme. Tinctoris, throughout his treatise on counterpoint —to select the central part of his work—uses not only phrases like these: such a procedure "offends the sophisticated ear";[16] or, in this procedure "the ear of the listener finds a modicum of sweetness";[17] but, also, "in the judgment of my ears."[18]

It is, of course, a truism that music, at all times, and also during the Middle Ages, was an art of the ear. That medieval theorists refer to the ear surely needs no documentation. To regard medieval music as governed by mathematics alone would be as wrongheaded as to consider Renaissance music as a matter of the ear alone. At all times there is a lively tension and interplay between the sensual and the intellectual, in music as well as in the other arts. The question is, What happens when demands of the ear conflict with those of mathematics? It is, however, not only a matter of which element prevails in case of conflict, but also how these elements are regarded. Medieval theorists speak of "the ear" as an objective entity—much as the scholastic speaks of "the Soul" or "the Intellect"—the Renaissance theorist not only distinguishes between a common ear and a sophisticated one, he begins to speak of "my ear." Personal experience now becomes a valid point of departure. Moreover, the Renaissance writer introduces a notion peculiarly absent in the medieval literature on music, the concept of aesthetic judgment. Finally, it is in the Renaissance that the conflict between the ear and mathematics in matters musical is not only openly acknowledged but often no less openly resolved in favor of the ear. These are fundamental differences. To gloss over them means to obscure the historical process, to do injustice to the individuality of two great epochs, and to deprive the history of theory of all power to account for the undeniably radical changes in the evolution of music itself.

For Tinctoris the chief distinction of the music of his day lay in its new wealth of consonances. Spreading over a full three octaves—exceeding the medieval range by three half tones —"modern" musicians had at their disposal no fewer than twenty-two consonances. Few commentaries are as revealing as that by Tinctoris when he sets out to justify this new abundance of consonances in modern compositions as against the "six" consonances of Boethius. They are, he says, approved in "Aristoxenian fashion by the judgment of the ear."[19] Now, in medieval and Renaissance theory alike, Pythagoras stood for the doctrine that music was subject to numbers, Aristoxenus for the opposing doctrine that the ear, not mathematical proportion, was decisive in matters of music.

One would have to go far afield to find a medieval theorist who would, in the crucial matter of consonances, give preference to Aristoxenian views over the time-honored Pythagorean sanction of consonance by mathematical proportion. This would already have been difficult because Aristoxenus had been thoroughly discredited by Boethius, whose authority in matters of music was unquestioned throughout the Middle Ages. Boethius had castigated Aristoxenus variously as the man "who left all judgment up to the ear,"[20] "who permitted everything to the judgment of the ear."[21] To him, he opposed Pythagoras, who "having left behind the judgment of the ear, having proceeded to the underlying causes, mistrusting any human ear"—now follows a description of the unreliability of the sense of hearing— "and setting no store by instruments"—here follows a catalogue of reasons for the unreliability of instruments—"inquired how one could explore the true cause of consonance through reason in a solid and reliable fashion."[22]

These words find their echo quite generally in medieval treatises on music.[23] Pythagoras is extolled, Aristoxenus is ignored or dismissed a "lending too much credence to the sense of hearing."[24] The fear of the eleventh-century [Pseudo-]-Bernelinus, "lest we leave this only to the judgment of the ear, and seem to approach Aristoxenus while being condemned by Boethius and the Pythagoreans,"[25] is characteristic of the medieval outlook.

We must recall this to appreciate the quiet revolution manifested in Tinctoris' words: "approved in Aristoxenian fashion by the judgment of the ear."[26]

Obviously, the Renaissance writers on music, a quarrelsome lot by any standards, did not suddenly agree on acclaiming Aristoxenus as their new patron saint—and this for many reasons: the immense weight and authority of the "official" tradition; the undiminished poetic glamor and philosophical appeal of the idea of music as an echo of the "harmony of the universe" and a sounding image of mathematical proportion; that Aristoxenus was identified not only with a general philosophy of music but with certain practical procedures such as equal temperament, which was a controversial issue throughout the Renaissance;[27] and last (but not least), the intellectual temper of men like Zarlino—to name the most important figure—who strove toward a harmonious compromise between the opposing doctrines.

When the center of gravity in theory shifts from mathematics to the sensual and aesthetic aspects of music, one may expect a concomitant reversal of the medieval view which placed theory on the top of the pyramid and practical music at the bottom. Indeed, Tinctoris now assigns the leading role in musical culture to the composer. In a gesture, the symbolic value of which cannot be missed, he dedicates his treatise on modes[28] to the two greatest composers of his time, Johannes Ockeghem and Antoine Busnois, chapelmasters of the King of France and the Duke of Burgundy, respectively. More novel yet is the recognition given to musical performers. The medieval theorist took, at best, a condescending view of the performer. Boethius had declared: "Physical practice is like a servant, but theory reigns like a lord." Following him, medieval theory reserved the title *musicus* for the speculative theorist; the *cantor*, on the other hand, was he who merely sang without deeper understanding of the foundations of music. He was, therefore, no better than a bird, a mere beast: "Nam qui facit, quod non sapit, diffinitur bestia." This is the conclusion of Guido of Arezzo's famous jingle on the difference between *musicus* and *cantor*.

All of this was in line with medieval philosophy, which distinguished between the *artes liberales* and the *artes serviles* or *mechanicae*. Since only the soul was considered free, any art exercised by the body was a servile, a mechanical, art.[29] Thus musical performance was on a par with navigation, hunting, weaving, which were, to the unceasing vexation of the artists, considered equal to drawing, painting, and sculpture.

It is, therefore, not customary for a medieval theorist to mention, let alone praise, musical performers. It is even rare, indeed quite exceptional, to find him discussing individual composers.

Tinctoris, on the other hand, made it fashionable for musical theorists to discuss and analyze specific works of specific composers and to mention and praise the merits of individual singers and instrumentalists. One may say that he created the beginnings of the concert review when he not only published a list of the greatest singers of his age[30] but proceeded to define the qualifications of a good singer in this order: art, rhythm, style, vocal rendering, and a good voice.[31]

If a good voice may be regarded as a physical attribute, art, rhythm, style, and vocal rendering have to do with matters of artistic judgment and execution. With this definition of good singing in which intellectual and physical attributes are mingled, Tinctoris brushes aside as meaningless both the traditional distinction between an *ars liberalis* and an *ars servilis* and that between the *musicus* and the *cantor*. This is evident, also, from Tinctoris' definition of *musicus* in his famous dictionary of musical terms. Although he still quotes Guido's rhyme, he explains that a "musician is he who assumes the office of singer after careful rational investigation through benefit of thought."[32] Tinctoris boldly undertook to merge the opposites of an old, invidious comparison into a new harmonious synthesis.[33]

Tinctoris also singles out great instrumental virtuosos for praise. The famous lutanist Pietro Bono, favorite at a number of Renaissance courts, is extolled for his skill in improvising embellishments on a given theme; the German Orbus, for his ability to play two, three, or four parts on the lute.[34]

A direct line leads from Tinctoris, Neapolitan by choice, to Luigi Dentice, native Neapolitan nobleman, who in his *Dialoghi* of 1553, written in the vernacular, describes a concert in the house of Donna Giovanna of Aragon, gives the names of the performers, their voices and instruments, and confesses that only few solo singers who accompany themselves on an instrument can please him, "because all of them are deficient in one or another regard: either in intonation, or in pronunciation, or in their accompaniment, or in their embellishment, or in their use of *crescendo* or *decrescendo* where needed: things acquired partly by art and partly by natural talent."[35]

The sophistication with which connoisseurs now judge the performer's art extends to the cultivated layman. Dentice is followed by the Florentine mathematician Cosimo Bartoli. In his *Ragionamenti accademici,* published in 1567, but written a good twenty years earlier, Bartoli gives accounts of the musicians of his time—composers, singers, instrumentalists—that are astonishingly acute in musical judgment. Interestingly enough, Bartoli agrees closely with Tinctoris' estimate of the rebirth of music; but writing seventy years after him, he dates it one generation later. He writes: "I am well aware that in his day Ockeghem was, as it were, the first to rediscover music then as good as dead, just as Donatello discovered sculpture in his; and that of Josquin, Ockeghem's pupil, one may say that he was a natural prodigy in music, just as our own Michelangelo Buonarotti has been in architecture, painting, and sculpture; for just as Josquin has still to be surpassed in his composition, so Michelangelo stands alone and without a peer among all who have practiced his arts; and the one and the other have opened the eyes of all who delight in these arts, now and in the future."[36]

THE NATURE OF THE NEW

We have returned, in a somewhat surreptitious fashion, to our point of departure, Tinctoris' praise of the music of his day as a new art and his dating of the origins of this new art as about 1435. What is the nature of the new art?

Writing in 1477, Tinctoris was witness to the first evolution of modern harmony and counterpoint, i.e., that harmony and that counterpoint which, in their essential outlines, have domi-

nated musical thought for almost half a millenium. In this sense
"modern harmony" is the art of concord based on the triad, and
"modern counterpoint" is the art of combining two, three, four,
five, and more voices in such a manner that the greatest melodic
and rhythmic freedom of each single voice may be obtained
in a carefully regulated harmonic sound texture. The classical
medieval technique of finishing one voice-part before adding
another, in which the harmonic sound was the result rather than
the clearly intended aim, gave way to a new compositional
technique in which all parts of a composition were conceived
and designed simultaneously in constant relation to one another.[37] Naturally, the harmonic result of the medieval technique
could not help but turn out to be haphazard, with dissonances
emerging often by chance. In the new technique of the Renaissance the euphony of the whole was planned in advance; and
the treatment of dissonance, for the first time in polyphonic
composition, was carefully designed as to the degree of sharp-
ness, its preparation and resolution, and its timing.

Comparison of a three-part chanson by the mature Dufay
(1400–74) with one by Machaut (1300–77) would show that
Dufay designs the parts in close association with one another so
that a euphonious harmonic whole results, whereas Machaut
lets them run merrily alongside one another, concerned only
that they should, at the conclusion of phrases, come together in
a perfect consonance or a triad, allowing any sort of dissonance
or parallel motion in octaves and fifths along the way. This
unconcern with regulated harmony struck the Renaissance ear
as so barbarous, and the Renaissance mind as so insufficient to
the demands of art, that Tinctoris could deny, with assurance
of complete approval, the existence of any music worth hearing

before 1430, roughly speaking, when, for the first time, harmony was made a primary goal of polyphonic organization.[38]

Tinctoris was fully aware of the new principles governing the *ars nova* of his time. Indeed, his treatise on counterpoint is the classic document of the new harmonic art and the new treatment of dissonance, and should more properly be called a treatise on harmony and counterpoint. Its three books deal in turn with consonances, dissonances, and eight rules of counterpoint. It is with pride that the Flemish-Italian theorist compares the richness of his twenty-two consonances with the poverty of the six consonances of Boethius.[39] To be sure, a long line of development led from Boethius to Tinctoris. Prosdocimo de Beldemandis, for example, in his small treatise on counterpoint written in 1412,[40] comes very close to Tinctoris' repertory of consonances even though he does not present it in such systematic form; and he was preceded by many others who liberalized Boethius' restricted scheme. But there is a significant distinction between Prosdocimo's and Tinctoris' explanation of the "imperfect" consonances. Prosdocimo, commenting on the intervals of the third and sixth and their "equivalents," the tenth and thirteenth, says: "they are called imperfect because the consonance which they render to the human ear, while good, is not perfect, but imperfect."[41] Tinctoris, playing on the double meaning of *perfectio* as "perfection" and as "cadence," i.e., the ending—and therefore the perfecting—of a musical phrase, says: "Perfect are those [consonances] through which, as the principal ones, and therefore more apt for this function, the cadences of each composition are constituted"—and now he enumerates the ten perfect consonances from the unison to the triple octave. "Imperfect are those through which, being less important and not fit for this function, no cadence can be effected in a composition,"[42] and now follows a list of the two thirds, two sixths, and their composites in the second and third octaves (twelve imperfect, and thus twenty-two consonances altogether).

Tinctoris throws overboard the whole notion that the ear distinguishes between perfect and imperfect consonances in the literal sense of these words. Holding fast to his point of departure, his own sense of hearing, and knowing full well the importance which thirds and sixths have in the composition of his day, he preserves the old terminology, while giving it a new definition. Thus he appears to be the first theorist who dismisses the traditional notion of "imperfect" consonances. But he does it in such a quiet way—and this distinguishes the Fleming from the fierce Spanish temperament of Ramos (of whom we shall hear presently)—that it went practically unnoticed.

Johannes Gallicus, Tinctoris' immediate predecessor, considers the thirds and sixths—and here he proves himself more old-fashioned than many a medieval writer—as not even worthy of the name of consonance; he calls them "dissonantiae compassibiles,"[43] ("tolerable dissonances"). Gallicus justifies his unusual classification in the orthodox medieval manner on the grounds of mathematical proportion.[44] In an earlier chapter, he speaks of the three perfect consonances, eulogizing the octave as a God-like consonance based on the perfect relationship of multiple ratio $1 : 2$. Fifth and fourth, based on the superparticular ratios $2 : 3$ and $3 : 4$—about which presently—lose in perfection to the same degree as they gain in distance from the simple multiple ratio of the octave. While this reasoning puts him squarely in the camp of the Pythagoreans and the ancient Greeks whose musical philosophy he wishes to restore and to apply to the "angelic" music of the Gregorian chant, it removes him effectively from the company of his contemporaries, particularly the composers of the despised counterpoint.

Although Tinctoris' theory of consonance is couched in the traditional form of a theory of intervals, i.e., consonances consisting of two tones only, two qualifications should be made.

First, in the medieval view an interval is a static phenomenon. Since the mathematical proportion for any interval is fixed, the character of the interval is likewise fixed. In Tinctoris' view the character of consonance can change according to its context. A single major sixth, for example, reckoned as dissonance by previous generations of musicians, strikes Tinctoris' ear still somewhat roughly; but set in a series of sixth chords and followed by the proper endings (of an octave or a tenth), the interval can be used with excellent results.[45] This again is a courageous acknowledgment of the superiority of the ear over mathematics in matters of music. Secondly, Tinctoris actually does treat the harmonic phenomenon of the triad, even though only indirectly. Discussing further the relative character of the sixth, he says that it can be transformed to unqualified sweetness when appearing in company of a third voice with either third and tenth, or, much better yet, with fifth or twelfth, i.e., as a triad in open position with the root in the bass.[46]

The new wealth of harmony described by Tinctoris was based not only on the different sensibilities of the Renaissance ear but also on the boldness of the Renaissance mind determined to recognize as consonances intervals such as the thirds and the sixths—felt to be consonant by the ear although according to Pythagorean mathematical theory no simple, i.e., multiple or superparticular, ratio existed for them.[47] A multiple ratio is the relationship of two numbers the larger of which contains a multiple of the smaller (1 : 2 , 1 : 3 , and so on). A superparticular ratio is the relationship of the two succeeding numbers. The relationship of a tone to its octave corresponds to the multiple ratio 1 : 2 ; a fifth corresponds to 2 : 3 , a fourth to 3 : 4 , both superparticular ratios. Now Renaissance theory—and I shall return to this later—put up the superparticular ratio 4 : 5 for the major, and 5 : 6 for the minor, third,[48] although from the Pythagorean (or strictly mathematical) point of view, these were not exact ratios but mere approximations. Zarlino codified the so-called *senario*—that is, the series of proportions from 1 : 2 to 5 : 6—as the mathematical origin of all harmony.[49]

This change in the mathematical formulas for the so-called imperfect consonances signified at once the spirit of criticism that dared deviate from the sacrosanct code of Pythagorean proportions and the belief in the reality of the theory of proportions as a life-giving principle of harmony. The theory of proportions was not rejected as opposed to experience; it was adjusted to experience. If one reads Zarlino's chapter "on the proprieties of the senary" and observes his procedure in sounding together all the intervals born from these relationships (i.e., octave, fifth, fourth, major third, minor third), "out of which emerge such harmony that the ear derives highest pleasure from it," one perceives that the Renaissance with regard to Pythagoras and Aristoxenus underwent Hegel's dialectic evolution of thesis, antithesis, synthesis. One also understands now why Zarlino calls the great Venetian composer Adrian Willaert, a native of Flanders and the professed model of his theoretical work, not a "new Aristoxenus," but a "new Pythagoras."[50] For, once the adoption of the Aristoxenian principle of the ear's leadership had brought about the acknowledgment of the thirds and sixths as consonances, and once the Pythagorean principle of the relationship between numerical proportion and consonance had been translated into the new "senario," the old marvel of the union of mathematics and harmony was not only revived but miraculously increased.

Unquestionably, Zarlino considered the synthesis of Pythagorean and Aristoxenian principles as a triumph of this theory. No doubt it satisfied the deepest aspirations of the Renaissance mind at its point of balance and maturity.

This interpretation is corroborated by Zarlino's mediating stand in the age-old question on the pre-eminence of reason over the senses or vice versa. Zarlino emphasizes the importance he attaches to his position in this problem by reserving its treatment for the last chapter of his work. His thought can best be summarized in his own words: "Senses without reason, reason without senses are equally powerless to deliver a solid judgment on whatever scientific problem; such judgment becomes possible when the two are joined together." [51] This is Zarlino's significant modification of the position of Boethius, [52] who declares the senses to be the obedient servant, but reason the judge and master.

Unlike Ramos, Zarlino did not trumpet his disagreement with Boethius, Guido, and the whole complex of medieval theory all over the world. But that he considered his own philosophy of music as a triumph over that of his predecessors, and inspired by the God of Music, he hinted unmistakably in the miniature illustration adorning the initial of his *Proemio*. The letter "M" with which his work begins stands for "Music" as well as for "Marsyas" who is shown lying on the ground, helpless, as Apollo begins to flay him—a hint the more significant as Zarlino seems to have been himself responsible for the publication of his first and greatest work: no printer's name is mentioned, and the printer's privilege of the Venetian Republic is granted to "Gioseffo Zarlino da Chioza." Besides, Zarlino underscores his intention by reserving the "Marsyas" miniature for the beginning of his work. Wherever else a chapter begins with the letter "M," [53] we see Mars holding Venus in passionate embrace, while the treacherous net descends upon the lovers.

Who is the Marsyas whom Zarlino wishes to be flayed? Indubitably, Nicola Vicentino, who also opens the first chapter of his work, *L'antica musica ridotta alla moderna prattica*, Rome, 1555 (about which later), with a large historiated initial showing a differently conceived scene of Apollo's flaying of Marsyas. The victim stands tied to a tree, with his arms raised above his shoulders. Apollo holds a knife in his right hand, in his left the skin of Marsyas' right arm. Behind Marsyas, on a branch of the tree, hangs his instrument, the panpipes; in Apollo's corner stands, slightly tilted, a stringed instrument, half viola da gamba, half lira da braccio, with only three strings. In the background is a round *tempietto,* a shrine undoubtedly dedicated to the god of the muses.

That Zarlino had Vicentino in mind when he opened his work published three years later with an initial depicting the same scene may be concluded from the fact that the last chapter of the third book offers an explicit and spirited rebuttal of Vicentino's ideas (see note 104).

BEGINNINGS OF AN AESTHETICS OF MUSIC

If Tinctoris' treatment of consonances marks the beginning of the Renaissance concept of harmony,[54] his treatise on counterpoint contains also the first formulation of aesthetic principles.

His eight rules of counterpoint culminate in the demand that "variety should be most diligently searched for in all counterpoint, for as Horace has it in his *Poetica:*[55] 'a harper is laughed at who always blunders on the same string.' As in the art of speech, in Cicero's opinion,[56] variety pleases the listener greatly, so also in polyphonic music diversity stimulates the listener's soul to intense enjoyment. Hence Aristotle, in his Ethics,[57] did not hesitate to assert that variety is a very pleasing thing and the nature of man stands in need of it."[58]

If variety, adopted as a conscious principle of aesthetics to govern all aspects of composition, is noteworthy in a fifteenth-century treatise on music, even more remarkable are the references to Horace's *De arte poetica*, to Cicero's *De oratore*, and to Aristotle's *Ethics*. Far from presenting the vanity of a Renaissance musician trying to impress his colleagues with learned quotations, these references are a serious and novel attempt to lift the discussion of musical composition from the level of a craft to that of an art that shares in the principles of other arts. Without mentioning it explicitly, Tinctoris, in elaborating upon the idea of *varietas*, introduces also the principle of *decorum*, well known from rhetoric and poetics, when he observes: "However, in all of this a sense of proportion is highly necessary . . . for the number and character of varieties that are suitable to a chanson are not the same ones that suit a motet, nor do those that are suitable to a motet befit a Mass."[59]

If Tinctoris was interested in the ideas of ancient Greek and Roman writers on rhetoric and literary style, we may certainly assume that he was curious about ancient Greek music. But two great obstacles confronted him and his contemporaries: no monuments of Greek music were known in his day, and Latin translations of Greek authors dealing with music were not as yet (when musicians still knew no Greek) generally available.[60] In the dedication of his *Proportionale* to King Ferdinand of Sicily, Tinctoris pays tribute to the great tradition of Greek music, he enumerates the names of famed Greek musicians, but then goes on to say: "Yet, we have no written tradition informing us how they performed or composed, but it is very likely that they did so with great elegance." [61]

However, there is one aspect of Greek music that fascinated Tinctoris as well as all other Renaissance musicians—curiously enough, it is one that almost all music historians of the last one hundred years have met with embarrassed silence, if not outright contempt. [62] This is the Greek theory and Greek legends concerning the psychological, and often miraculous, effects of music. Tinctoris himself wrote a treatise entitled *Complexus effectuum musices,* [63] which he dedicated to Beatrice of Aragon. With the thoroughness peculiar to his Flemish turn of mind, he enumerated twenty effects of music, describing each one of them in a separate chapter and proving their truth with a whole corpus of quotations in which Solomon and David, St. Augustine and St. Thomas Aquinas find themselves in the company of Aristotle and Vergil, Horace and Ovid, Cicero and Quintilian. He concluded his treatise with these words: "He who studies these effects will never regret having applied his talent to this branch of the [musical] discipline. On the contrary, he will, with burning enthusiasm, daily increase his study of that music, which kings, which other princes, and which free men have used, and which brought them commendation and glory! This is the music approved and taught by Lycurgus, Plato, Quintilian. He who follows their teachings shall never fail the art nor shall the ornament of art ever fail him." [64]

Franchino Gafori who, as a young man, spent two years in Naples with Tinctoris and later served at the court of Milan together with Leonardo da Vinci, and who followed Johannes Gallicus in proudly cultivating a humanistic Latin style, opened his *Theorica musicae* of 1480, his first publication, with a long and elaborate chapter on the effects of music.[65] Whereas Tinctoris still distinguished between Christianity and the *falsa religio*[66] of the Romans, Gafori relates the miracles effected by Orpheus, Amphion, Arion, Timotheus, and countless other Greek musicians with the religious awe of the true humanist.

Even that hard-bitten Spanish skeptic Bartolomeo Ramos, whose sarcastic attacks on Guido of Arezzo, patron saint of medieval music, aroused the ire of generations of theorists, especially his own, when it came to these wonder stories, said: "However fabulous and incredible they appear, there is no doubt that music works miracles."[67] Mentioning by name the legendary Greek musicians, he remarked: "It was these whom the venerable antiquity so admired that they were said to move wild beasts through the sweetness of their song, to capture the hearts of men, to revive the dead, to bend to mercy the spirits of the underworld, to draw trees from the mountains."[68] And he added: "Without a doubt, music has immense effect upon and mighty power over the human soul, whether to calm or to rouse it. If in our time music does not work so many miracles, it is to be attributed not to the art, whose perfection exceeds that of Nature, but to those who use the art badly. If those excellent [Greek] musicians whom we remembered above were called back to life they would deny that our music was invented by them—so inept, unharmonious, and dissipated has it been rendered through the corruption of certain singers."[69]

The fascination of the Renaissance with the "effects" of music, as mirrored in a vast literature of writings on music[70] as well as in a special poetic genre, the *laudes musicae*,[71] is much more than a curiosity to be excused with the naïve credulity of this humanistic age for anything ancient;[72] it is in essence a symbol of the transformation of music from a handmaid of theology to the most human art imaginable because it affects man's soul more profoundly and more immediately than any other art.[73] The fabled effects upon stones, trees, animals, and even the ancient deities are only an extension of the effect that music exercises over man. This is the significance of the ever-repeated legends of Orpheus' victory over the furies and the gods of the underworld,[74] or of Timotheus' power over Alexander in alternately rousing him from table to warring passion and calming him again to convivial merriment.[75]

The preoccupation with the "effects" of music is unquestionably connected with one of the most fateful changes in the orientation of the musical art. If Timotheus could arouse contrasting passions in Alexander, he did so by the use of contrasting musical means. To duplicate the ancient effects meant to the Renaissance composer that he had to rediscover the varying musical means that would produce these effects.

In other words, should music have the power of tuning man's soul to cheer, it had to express cheerfulness; should it arouse him to war, it had to express warlike feelings; if it was to lead him to melancholy, it had to express sadness. Already Ramos was stung by the failure of contemporary music to equal the effects of Greek music. In the opinion of an ever increasing number of Renaissance musicians, this failure was due to the lack of expressive power in the music of their time.[76]

If the composers were to succeed in developing the expressive vein of music, they would have to free themselves increasingly from technical considerations blocking their free invention. This is, I believe, the chief reason for the emancipation of Renaissance polyphony from *cantus-firmus* technique, from the strictures of canonic writing, from the artifice of rhythmic proportions. In a *cantus-firmus* work the composer selected a pre-existent melody, liturgical or secular, for the tenor part while using the other voices to build a contrapuntal edifice over this foundation. Hence the composer's imagination was restricted not only in the tenor part, but in the conception of the whole, since all parts are tied to the tenor. In a composition based on simple or multiple canon, the invention of melody was determined and restricted by the need to have that same melody imitated in other voices without violating the laws of harmony and counterpoint. In a work based on the play with rhythmic proportions, each voice may go under its own time signature, or the single voices themselves may engage in changing meters while constantly conflicting with the meter of all other voices. Here the rhythmic life of the music is mathematically predetermined and thus the composer has no freedom to adjust his rhythm to expressive purposes. The place of these techniques in shaping musical form was now taken over by the poetic text, the composer's imagination being directed more and more by the pictorial and emotional content of the words.[77]

It is this change of which Adrian Petit Coclico in his *Compendium musices* of 1552 speaks when he admonishes the young musician "not to waste his time on the lengthy writings of musical mathematicians, who contrived so many categories of augmentation and diminution signs, from which proceeds no enjoyment, but quarrel and discord in plenty, and through which a thing clear in itself is rendered obscure. Rather let them apply all mental energies to sing ornately, to place the text well, for Music is created by God not for quarreling, but for its sweet sound. In truth, the musician is he, and is held to be he, who rather than chatter and scribble a lot on numbers and proportions, on signs and note values, knows how to sing tastefully and sweetly, giving each note its appropriate syllable, and how to compose so as to render joyful words in joyful tones and vice versa, etc."[78]

One hundred years earlier, Johannes Gallicus, the Carthusian monk, had issued a similar warning against the artifices of an overly complex counterpoint, but his alternative was a return to the simplicity of the plain chant and to the cultivation of music for the single purpose of the divine service. Now, Coclico, a Flemish Catholic turned Protestant, condemned the mathematical intricacies of Netherlandish polyphony with no less zeal, but the alternative is a music designed to please a human audience, as far as performance is concerned, and to express the emotions of the text as far as composition is concerned.

If the composer was to express the emotions of the words, he needed, in the first place, emotional texts. In the fifteenth century the Mass, with its ancient hallowed unchanging words, had been the mainstay of religious music; the late fifteenth and the sixteenth centuries turned increasingly to the motet, in which the composer was free to select any part of the Old or the New Testament as well as any part of the Breviary, and even secular texts, for polyphonic settings. The emotional language of the psalms, the impassioned tone of the love poems in the Song of Solomon, the most moving scenes from the Old Testament—David weeping over Jonathan, David lamenting Absalom, Job's despair, innocent Susanna condemned to death— and even, from the *Aeneid,* Dido's lament; all of these are new topics in Renaissance music; and their representation elicited new tones from the old lyre.[79]

By common acclaim of his contemporaries, Josquin des Prez (*ca.* 1440–1521) exceeded all other composers in the art of endowing the old counterpoint with the novel spirit of expressiveness. All writers of his time remark on this, none more poignantly than the Swiss humanist, musician, and theorist of music, Henricus Glareanus. In his *Dodekachordon,* published in 1547 but completed in 1540, he pays this tribute to Josquin: "No one has more effectively expressed the passions of the soul in music than this symphonist, no one has more felicitously begun, no one has been able to compete in grace and facility on an equal footing with him, just as there is no Latin poet superior in the epic to Maro. For just as Maro, with his natural facility, was accustomed to adapt his poem to his subject so as to set weighty matters before the eyes of his readers with close-packed spondees, fleeting ones with unmixed dactyls, to use words suited to his every subject, in short, to undertake nothing inappropriately, as Flaccus says of Homer, so our Josquin, where his matter requires it, now advances with impetuous and precipitate notes, now intones his subject in long-drawn tones, and, to sum up, has brought forth nothing that was not delightful to the ear, nothing, in short, that was not acceptable and pleasing, even when it seemed less erudite, to those who listened with judgment."[80]

And in commenting on one of Josquin's most expressive works, his lament of David on Jonathan, Glareanus remarks: ". . . Throughout the motet there is preserved what befits the mourner, who is wont at first to cry out frequently, then to murmur to himself, turning little by little to sorrowful complaints, thereupon to subside or sometimes, when passion breaks out anew, to raise his voice again, shouting a cry . . . by the gods, he has everywhere expressed the passion in a wonderful way, thus, at the very beginning of the tenor at the word 'Jonathan.'"[81]

When Tinctoris compared polyphonic music to rhetoric and

poetics, he did so on a level of abstraction, discussing the general principle of variety and its proper use in various genres of music. Glareanus, however, in comparing Josquin with Vergil, does so with regard to the power of the poet and the composer to express emotion in verse or in tones.

I should like to draw attention to a fleeting phrase in Glareanus' eulogy of Josquin: "nothing . . . that was not . . . pleasing, even when it seemed less erudite." Josquin was unexcelled in his mastery of contrapuntal artifice. But often when concentrating on problems of expression, he relaxed his attention to problems of contrapuntal complexity,[82] and some of Josquin's most expressive works, such as his cycle of passion motets, are written in a polyphonic style of great simplicity.[83]

CONFLICT BETWEEN THE SECULAR AND THE SACRED

Music, to acquire, increase, and refine its power of expressiveness, had to engage in a double process of loosening old ties, removing old rules, and adding new sonorities and new ways of organizing sounds. This explains why the sixteenth century is the age of experimentation par excellence.

It is not surprising that many of these experiments were inspired by the continued study of Greek musical theory. The Greeks' use of the chromatic scale with its succession of two semitones and the enharmonic scale with its succession of two quarter-tones intrigued the humanists of the Renaissance as well as the musicians, connoisseurs and amateurs as much as the professionals.

To introduce the chromatic and enharmonic genders into the polyphonic music of the time, the whole edifice of medieval musical theory had to be razed and a new structure put in its place. It is not by chance that the first man to experiment with the Greek genders was the same one who attacked the venerable tradition of Guido of Arezzo's system of solmization, deriding the founder of medieval theory with a tone of anticlerical irreverence unheard of in the Middle Ages as "perhaps a better monk than musician."[84] I refer to Bartolomeo Ramos, who replaced Guido's six-tone system with one of eight tones and thus made superfluous the whole complicated system of mutations,[85] who used a complete chromatic scale, recognized thirds and sixths as consonances, assigning them the simple ratios of 4 : 5 and 5 : 6, introduced significant changes in tuning, had already a notion of practical temperament,[86] and advocated a rich use of chromatic notes in performance on the part of the singers, thus revitalizing the old practice of *musica ficta*.

One could hardly imagine two reformers of more opposed temperaments than Tinctoris and Ramos. The Fleming, a clear-headed and resolute thinker, was nevertheless conciliatory and diplomatic in method. When he infused the old terms with new meaning, he was perhaps not following the Evangelist's direction about new wine and old bottles. He did so well with the old bottles that much of the novelty of the contents remained one of the best preserved secrets in the history of music theory. Ramos, on the other hand, was a pugnacious man. "I don't fear a fight," said he, "if it will be waged in the presence and under the arbitration of Reason."[87] But aside from a keen mind, he also had a sharp tongue. When he attacked Hothby, for example, he added insult to injury by concluding his argument with words that reduced the opponent to a mere shadow of Guido: "But I am not surprised, for he is a follower of Guido. I wish to destroy the head, so that the whole body of errors becomes a corpse and cannot live any longer."[88] Nor could his antitheological attitudes fail to make enemies. He refuted the validity of the venerable argument that the perfection of the ternary meter lay in the trinity of the divine persons and the intellective soul with the observation, "It is a defect to want to prove something in mathematical disciplines through analogy." [89] What Ramos wanted was obviously a theory of music as an autonomous field of secular learning freed from all theological ties and consideration. For this the time was not ripe.

It is not surprising then that the counterattack was opened and sustained by churchmen scandalized by the unrestrained vehemence of Ramos' fulminations against Guido and the whole system of medieval theory. Nicolaus Burtius, who published the first pamphlet "against a Spanish prevaricator of the truth" [90] in 1487, called himself on the title page, not only a professor of music, but also a student of pontifical law. A priest himself, [91] he dedicated his treatise to the *pauperibus clericis ac religiosis,* and he cites the authority of *Mater Ecclesia* for the retention of the diatonic and the rejection of the chromatic and enharmonic genders that Ramos wished to revive. [92] For Guido's teaching, including the whole system of solmization denounced by Ramos, he claims nothing less than divine inspiration—nay, command. [93]

John Hothby, the most objective of Ramos' critics, was a Carmelite; Gafori, a priest. The lone defender of Ramos, loyal to the end, was the keen-minded, mordant Bolognese, Giovanni Spataro, the first layman to become choirmaster of the Basilica of San Petronio. If the heat with which this controversy was conducted has been incomprehensible to music historians from Ambros on, it is, I believe, because it has not been realized that implied in it was the much larger issue of music as a secular art and discipline versus music as a servant of the liturgy. As art, Ramos thought, secular music ought to be the equal of church music. As theoretical discipline, music ought to be built on a rational foundation free from theological considerations.

This was the new position, and Ramos himself was quite clear about this aspect of his struggle. When he proposes to substitute for Guido's tone system his enlarged system of three octaves based on C, he does so "that it be of utility not only to ecclesiastical, but also the more curious secular music."[95] The old theory from Gregory to Guido is the law of Scripture, his new theory is the law of grace; many practice music without benefit of the former, but his new system embraces both arts, sacred and secular, and both laws, that of the Scriptures and that of nature.[96]

Nothing could show more clearly in which direction Ramos was moving than this opposition of the law of nature to that of the Scriptures.

Burtius, too, was keenly aware that the struggle was concerned with more than the question of solmization syllables. He recognized that the whole foundation of church music was beginning to shake under Ramos' onslaught. This is why he dedicated his treatise to the clergy, and why he harped constantly on Ramos' arrogance in the face of ecclesiastical tradition: "If Gregory wished to use only these seven Latin letters [a, b, c, . . .] and repeat them as often as needed, and if Ambrose and Augustine preferred to follow in his footsteps rather than in foreign ones, why don't you blush to pervert this order and deprave it with your arrogant censorship? Are you perhaps more saintly than these pillars of the Church or more cultivated or more experienced? . . . The doctrine of that pious monk, spread throughout the world, will last forever, notwithstanding your malice, partly because of the Church's approbation, partly because of the marvelous invention of the notes." [97]

Although Ramos had to leave Bologna, although his teachings were condemned by a formidable array of authorities, although Ramos himself never published anything else after the treatise of 1482, not even the second part of it that he had promised in this work, the movement that he had set into motion could not be stopped. For some time it seemed to go underground. The most important writings dealing with the new theories were not published,[98] the most astonishing compositional experiments remained isolated or in manuscript[99]—but both the writings and the experiments prove that the fermentation once begun never ceased. That it succeeded finally in transforming the whole fabric of music is proven by the appearance, in 1555, of one of the most radical treatises on music of all times: Nicola Vicentino's *L'antica musica ridotta alla moderna prattica.*[100]

This treatise, a systematic theory of composition and performance, not only advocates the use of all chromatic semitones and of quarter-tones in imitation of the Greeks and describes a new instrument built by its author that had thirty instead of twelve tones to the octave, it embodied the first aesthetics of expression, so radical in its application that it permitted anything prohibited before, as long as it served the cause of expression. Even the leap of a tritone, the interval generally tabooed in musical theory, was admitted by Vicentino for the sake of expressing an extraordinary conceit.[101]

Needless to say, Vicentino was attacked no less violently than was Ramos. But the time was farther advanced and Vicentino had what Ramos lacked, a powerful patron, and a cardinal at that, in Yppolito d'Este of Ferrara. The strongest opponent of Vicentino was Zarlino, the celebrated Venetian theorist, who, three years after Vicentino, published the most comprehensive, balanced, and judicious treatise of the century: the *Istitutioni harmoniche*. It is significant for the great changes described that Zarlino and Vicentino agree on the principle of text expression as the guiding consideration for the composer,[102] that they disagree only on the extent to which this principle should be carried. Zarlino upheld a concept of intrinsic musical beauty: he allowed presentation of strong emotions only as long as the music "does not offend the ear"—a statement that is curiously remindful of one by Mozart, two hundred and twenty-five years later, to the effect that "passions, whether violent or not, must never be expressed to the point of tedium, and music, even in the most dreadful (dramatic) situation, should never offend the ear, but should still please even then, hence should always remain music."[103] For Vicentino there was no such consideration. Zarlino opposed the extremes of Vicentino's theory, his chromaticism, his microtones, his new intervals, and his dissonance treatment.[104]

ALBERTI AND TINCTORIS: A COMPARISON

In conclusion I should like to suggest the strong parallel between developments in Renaissance music and Renaissance painting by comparing Tinctoris's book on counterpoint with Alberti's tract on painting.[105]

Significant is the coincidence between Tinctoris' *ars nova,* the birthdate of which is fixed by him as *circa* 1435, and Leon Battista Alberti's epoch-making treatise *Della pittura*, the date of which is 1436. As Tinctoris, in the struggle between the superiority of mathematics versus the ear, decides for the ear, so does Alberti for the eye when he, in the beginning of his treatise, writes: "In all this discussion, I beg you to consider me not as a mathematician but as a painter writing of these things.

Mathematicians measure with their minds alone the forms of things separated from all matter. Since we wish the object to be seen, we will use a more sensate wisdom." [106]

Alberti's treatise presents the first theory of perspective which Erwin Panofsky has defined as the "perfect unification and systematization of three-dimensional space." [107] In this new concept of pictorial space, to quote another art historian, "the new role of the spectator in relation to the picture . . . reflects the growing humanism of the period." [108]

The new Renaissance polyphony unifies the various inter-vallic layers of counterpoint into one coherent harmonic body; all musical phenomena must find their justification in the ear. Man takes a central position in both the new visual and musical art. Like Tinctoris, Alberti dedicates his work to a living artist, Brunelleschi; like Tinctoris, he quotes ancient authors, praises ancient art, and stresses the effects of painting upon man. "Painting contains," he says, "a divine force which not only makes absent men present . . . but moreover makes the dead seem almost alive. . . . Plutarch says that Cassander, one of the captains of Alexander, trembled through all his body because he saw a portrait of his King. . . . They say that Phidias made in Aulis a god Jove so beautiful that it consider-ably strengthened the religion then current." [109]

Alberti, like Tinctoris, stresses the principle of variety: "In food and in music novelty and abundance please, as they are different from the old and usual. So the soul is delighted by all copiousness and variety. For this reason copiousness and variety please in painting." [110] Alberti discusses the uses of variety in the number and difference of personages, of poses and motions, and of color. The principle of selection is *decorum* or *con-venienza*. "The painting ought to have pleasant and graceful movements, suitable to what is happening there. The movements and poses of virgins are airy, full of simplicity, with sweetness of quiet rather than strength. . . . In men the movements are more adorned with firmness, with beautiful and artful poses. In the old the movements and poses are fatigued. . . . "[111] As they praise variety, both Alberti[112] and Tinctoris[113] also warn against repetitiousness. Of course, in all of this Alberti precedes Tinctoris as Renaissance painting precedes Renaissance music in the portrayal of emotions of which Alberti says: "We painters . . . wish to show the movements of the soul by movements of the body. . . . "[114]

While the representation of the reality of man and the world receives attention of unprecedented intensity in Renaissance painting and music, while eye and ear attain to a position of unrivaled dominance in their respective arts, the ancient idea of mathematical proportion was by no means set aside; on the contrary, as Panofsky has pointed out, "the theory of proportions achieved an unheard-of prestige in the Renaissance. The proportions of the human body were praised as the visual realization of musical harmony."[115] But Panofsky shows that this theory was thoroughly revolutionized by "three forms of subjectivity" for the first time legitimized by the Renaissance: organic movement, perspective foreshortening, and the regard for the visual impression of the beholder. "Organic movement introduces . . . the subjective will and the subjective emotions of the thing represented; foreshortening the subjective visual experience of the artist; and those 'eurhythmic' adjustments which alter that which is right in favor of that which seems right, the subjective visual experience of a potential beholder."[116]

It is uncanny how precisely these changes are echoed in the music of the Renaissance. To start from the end: the change of the Pythagorean proportion 64 : 81 for the interval of the third to 64 : 80 = 4 : 5 can hardly be better described than a "eurhythmic" adjustment which alters that which is right in favor of that which sounds right. The subjective auditory experience of the artist led from polyphony as an organization of several layers of intervals, loosely connected, to a unified organization of harmony,[117] and from there, in slow stages, to tonality, a system in which all harmonies are related to a single harmonic point, the tonic, from which they receive their relative position in the harmonic space.[118] Finally, "the subjective will and the subjective emotions of the thing represented" that led a Michelangelo, according to his own statement, to interest himself less in numerical measurements than in the observation of *atti e gesti*, led a Josquin des Prez and his followers from a literal observation of the lawful consonances and dissonances to the expression of an ever-widening scale of human emotions involving novel sonorities such as modulation, chromaticism, and treatment of dissonance with increasing boldness.

The question of tradition and innovation in the Renaissance must needs be answered differently in the various fields of inquiry. New ideas and conceptions cannot be expected to begin in all branches of human creativity at the same time. But such phenomena as the discovery of perspective in painting, harmony in music, and the new language of emotion that slowly transformed both of these arts to give us the great masterworks of European painting and music are so fundamental and so new, and they come from such deep springs of human consciousness, that we may regard them as symbols of the dawn of a new era.

1. *Renaissance and Renascences in Western Art* (Stockholm, 1960), p. 5.
2. In an exemplary edition of his letters by Claude V. Palisca, Girolamo Mei has been revealed as the true fountainhead of the Camerata and mentor

of Galilei (*Girolamo Mei: Letters on Ancient and Modern Music to Vincenzo Galilei and Giovanni Bardi* [Rome, 1960]).

3. The same is true for the evolution of music itself. See my study on "Music in the Culture of the Renaissance," *Journal of the History of Ideas,* XV (1954), 509–53, 543–46.

4. *Liber de arte contrapuncti* (*Scriptorum de musica medii aevi,* ed. Coussemaker, Vol. IV [Paris, 1876]), p. 77*b* (hereinafter cited as Couss. IV). The above translation follows Oliver Strunk, *Source Readings in Music History* (New York, 1950), p. 199. As this paper was being prepared for publication, an English translation of the treatise by Albert Seay appeared as Number 5 of the series "Musicological Studies and Documents" (American Institute of Musicology, 1961). Unfortunately, the translation is in parts awkward, in parts incomprehensible, and in parts wrong. Before we have translations, we need a critical text.

5. Tinctoris is not the first writer on music to speak of "moderni." Particularly the introduction of mensural notation around 1300 caused so sharp a break between the *ars antiqua* and *ars nova* that the term "moderni" with reference to the composers as well as theorists becomes complementary to the designation *ars nova.* Theorists now use it with varying overtones of resentment or approval according to their points of view. One can find it time and time again in the treatises of Jacobus of Liége, *Speculum musicae,* ed. Roger Bragard (*Corpus scriptorum de musica* [Rome, 1955]), and of Marchettus of Padua, *Pomerium,* ed. Joseph Vecchi (*Corpus scriptorum de musica,* Vol. VI [Rome, 1961]), the former usually frowning, the latter smiling, at the *moderni.*

6. Couss. IV, 154*b*: " . . . Novae artis fons et origo, apud Anglicos quorum caput Dunstaple . . . et huic contemporanei fuerunt in Gallia Dufay et Binchois quibus immediate successerunt moderni Okeghem, Busnois, Regis et Caron, omnium quos audiverim in compositione praestantissimi."

7. *Ibid.*: "Illi etenim in dies novos cantus novissime inveniunt, ac isti (quod miserrimi signum est ingenii) una semper et eadem compositione utuntur."

8. Couss. IV, 299*a*: "Gallia namque me genuit et fecit cantorem. Ytalia vero qualemcunque sub Victorino Feltrensi, viro tam litteris graecis quam latinis affatim imbuto, grammaticum et musicum." The first scholar to draw attention to Gallicus' study under Vittorino da Feltre was P. O. Kristeller in his article on "Music and Learning in the Early Italian Renaissance," *Journal of Renaissance and Baroque Music,* I (1947), 255–74, 266–67.

9. Couss. IV, 369*a*: "Quis, oro, scire non debeat nullam prorsus ante Nostri Salvatoris adventum de plano cantu factam esse mentionem, huncque nobis christianis Angelicum ac tantae gravitatis canendi ritum a Spiritu Sancto postea magis quam ab hominibus traditum?"

10. *Voces frangere* refers to what we would now call "florid counterpoint." The fifteenth-century *Ars contrapunctus secundum Philippum de Vitriaco* distinguishes between *contrapunctus, id est nota contra notam* (Couss. III, 23*a*) and *cantus fractibilis in minoribus notis* (ibid., p. 27*a*). Likewise, Prosdocimo de Beldemandis (*Tractatus de contrapuncto,* Couss. III, 193 ff.) differentiates between *contrapunctus . . . stricte sumptus* which he defines as "unius solius note contra aliquam aliam unicam solam notam in aliquo cantu positio" (*ibid.,* p. 194*a*), in which dissonances are prohibited, and *cantus fractibilis,* which can take dissonances, "eo quod in ipso propter velo-

citatem vocum earum non sentiuntur dissonantie" (*ibid.*, p. 197*a*). Obviously, Gallicus' *voces frangere* is the same as Shakespeare's "division" ("Some say, the lark makes sweet division," *Romeo and Juliet*, III, v, 29), a term still used in the seventeenth century and defined in Christopher Simpson's *Division-Viol* of 1665 (see the facsimile edition [London, 1955], p. 27) as "the Breaking, either of the *Bass,* or of any higher *Part.* . . . "

11. Couss. IV, 344*a* and 344*b*: " . . . in variis cyfris ac diversis signis et caracteribus novos tota die cantus lascivose vanos exequentes totque stultas adinventiones in suis quas non intelligunt proportionibus phantasticantes. Quippe qui novunt cantus, quos mensuratos appellant, cyfris ac novis phantasiis adeo plenos sepius fabricare, quod nec ipsi, qui fecere, valent illos ut plurimum enuntiare, quos nihilominus laudant, in re tam vilissima, quasi magnum quod egerint, gloriantes. Quaenam haec vestra dementia cantores! Numquid haec tam nobilis scientia vestris erit subdita cyfris? Absit. Canite quaeso, canite. Voces quantum licet frangite, novas quotidie cantilenas suaves et tinnulas excogitate, tempus circa longas breves semibreves ac minimas consumite. Nam cum haec omnia perfecte nec aliud noveritis non dico quidem musici, sed neque veri cantores estis."

12. Couss. IV, 382*b*: "Verum quia vos [emended from Coussemaker's *nos*] magis delectat, o cantores mei, vulgo quam deo vestro canere, vos inquam vanitas illo permittente seducit, ligat ac inebriat cum vestris vanis cantibus, nam ingenium ibi valet, ubi mens intendit. Et nemo duobus dominis teste deo bene servivit, inquam."

13. Having praised Boethius' *musica,* Gallicus continues (Couss. IV, 300*a*): "Mei namque propositi non est theoricam hujus artis velle post tam eximium virum, nisi forsan raro coactus tractare quin potius veram priscorum ecclesiae Christi praticam; quae tota nihilominus ab illo fonte [Boetii] procedit, si possim renovare."

14. Couss. IV, 346*a*: "Sed non patri Gregorio placuit haec lascivia." These words are echoed in Bartolomeo Ramos' *Musica practica* of 1482 (see the edition of Wolf [Leipzig, 1901], p. 9): "Sed nec Gregorio placuit litterae additio, quoniam quindecim tantum usus est." On Gallicus as a predecessor of Ramos, see Edward E. Lowinsky, "The Concept of Physical and Musical Space in the Renaissance," *Papers of the American Musicological Society,* 1941 (1946), pp. 57–84, 75–76.

15. It goes without saying that a Renaissance writer speaking of man usually thinks of him as unburdened by the toil and sweat that is the foundation of life; he thinks of the free man who can devote himself to the higher things, and that means in particular to the seven liberal arts (see note 29, below). Thus, when Tinctoris dedicates a treatise to his royal disciple, Beatrice of Aragon, he expresses the hope she may find that he taught in it something worthy of a free man: "si in eo me libero homine digna precepisse [emended from Coussemaker's *percepisse*] inveneris."—Couss. IV, 47*a*.

16. " . . . Aures eruditas offendit."—Couss. IV, 111*a*.

17. " . . . Modicum suavitudinis sensus auditoris percipit."—*Ibid.*, p. 111*b*.

18. " . . . Aurium mearum judicio."—*Ibid.*, p. 88*a*.

19. Couss. IV, 79*b*: " . . . ad istas 22 concordantias me restrinxi, quas aevi praesentis compositores cantoresque priscis multo praestantiores, more Aristoxeni aurium judicio comprobatas, in usum assumpserunt. . . . "

20. *Boetii de institutione musica*, ed. G. Friedlein (Leipzig, 1867), p. 267: "Aristoxenus . . . qui auribus dedit omne iudicium. . . . "

21. *Ibid.*, p. 268: " . . . Aristoxenus musicus, iudicio aurium cuncta permittens. . . . "

22. *Ibid.*, pp. 196–97: " . . . relicto aurium iudicio Pythagoras ad regularum momenta migraverit, qui nullis humanis auribus credens . . . nullis etiam deditus instrumentis . . . inquirebat, quanam ratione firmiter et constanter consonantiarum momenta perdisceret."

23. Sometimes they are literally quoted as in the *Tractatus de musica* by Hieronymus de Moravia, ed. P. Dr. Simon M. Cserba, O.P. (Regensburg, 1935), p. 123.

24. Thus, for example, Jacobus of Liége in his *Speculum musicae*, Bk. II, p. 102: " . . . Aristoxenus, qui nimis sensui credidit. . . . "

25. "Bernelini cita et vera divisio monochordi" (Gerbert, *Scriptores ecclesiastici de musica sacra potissimum*, I, 314*a*–*b*: " . . . ne iudicio tantum aurium illud committamus, et Aristoxeno proximare videamur, a Boëtio autem & Pythagoricis condemnemur.")

26. Seay's supposition (*The Art of Counterpoint*, p. 5) "that Tinctoris did not realize all the implications of his own approaches to music theory, that he was, in a certain sense, a revolutionary writer" becomes in this context of ideas completely unthinkable.

27. See Edward E. Lowinsky, "Adrian Willaert's Chromatic 'Duo' Reexamined," *Tijdschrift voor Muziekwetenschap*, XVIII (1956), 1–36, 7–13. There I examined the question of equal temperament associated by Renaissance writers with Aristoxenus' theorem that the octave is divisible into six whole-tone steps. Interestingly enough, Tinctoris, in the same treatise, refers to the Aristoxenian division of the octave into six whole tones (Couss. IV, p. 91) and to Boethius' refutation of it. If Tinctoris had had any practical musical reason for siding in this question with Aristoxenus against Boethius, I am inclined to think that he would not have hesitated to do so. But the time of the chromatic experiments, when equal temperament became a practical necessity, was still in the future.

28. *Liber de natura et proprietate tonorum* (Couss. IV, 16–41).

29. See Edgar de Bruyne, *Etudes d'esthétique médiévale* (3 vols.; Bruges, 1946), II, 385 ff. For Thomas Aquinas' views on *artes liberales* and *artes serviles*, see *ibid.*, III, 335 ff.

30. See Karl Weinmann, *Johannes Tinctoris und sein unbekannter Traktat "De usu et inventione musicae"* (Regensburg, 1917), p. 33 (a reprint of this book has been edited by W. Fischer [Tutzing, 1961]). Weinmann discovered in the Proske Music Library at Regensburg the unique copy of an incunabulum, printed in Naples in the year 1487, containing a few chapters of a work on the use and the invention of music that has been lost. The print of 1487

was, as it were, a sample from the book offered to his friend, the composer Johannes Stokem. The title, stressing two aspects of music usually neglected in medieval treatises, practice and history, and also the few chapters preserved show that we have suffered a grievous loss in the disappearance of this work. The chapters preserved, in which Tinctoris, following Horace's injunction, "mingled the sweet with the useful" ("dulci utile miscui") show an enchanting combination of practical lore, particularly concerning the instrumentarium of his time, and humanistically inspired ancient history of music and instruments written in by far the most elegant Latin found in any of his treatises. Unquestionably, this was the most humanistic, the most secular of Tinctoris' treatises; even Christ appears in it like a Christian Apollo. Here Tinctoris comes very close to the humanistic style and manner of Gafori, whose first work was published in 1478 in Naples, where he spent two years (1478-80) enjoying the stimulating company of the Flemish musician.

31. *Ibid.*: " . . . ars: mensura: modus: pronunciatio: et vox bona." The term "modus" refers here certainly not to mensural notation but to style of melody and of singing. In this manner St. Augustine uses the term in his *Confessions* in a passage quoted by Tinctoris in his treatise on modes (Couss. IV, 19a): "omnes affectus spiritus nostri pro sua diversitate habent proprios modos in voce atque cantu . . . " ("all affects of our soul have in accordance with their diversity their proper styles in voice and song."). The term "pronunciatio" is defined in Tinctoris' *Terminorum musicae diffinitorium*, ed. Armand Machabey (Paris, 1951), p. 43, and in Couss. IV, 186b, as "venusta vocis emissio."

32. A. Machabey, *op. cit.*, p. 39; Couss. IV, 186a: "Musicus est qui perpensa ratione beneficio speculationis, canendi officium assumit." The words "non operis servitio" ("not in the service of practice") following in Coussemaker and Machabey after "speculationis" do not occur in the original print; they appear only in the Brussels manuscript followed by Coussemaker. They would serve to sharpen the antithesis between theory and practice that Tinctoris attempts to soften.

33. This escaped Seay who—after a correct exposition of Tinctoris' lack of interest in abstract speculation—says (*The Art of Counterpoint*, p. 5): "It is curious, on the other hand, that Tinctoris gives in his *Diffinitorium* the old, old definition of the musician, that taken over directly from Boetius [*sic*] and Guido. . . . "

34. See Karl Weinmann, *op. cit.*, p. 35.

35. *Duo dialoghi della musica del Signor Luigi Dentice gentil' huomo Napolitano* (Rome, 1553), "Dialogo secondo," H3v: "Perche tutti errano in qualche cosa, o nella intonatione, o nella pronunciatione, o nel sonare, o nel fare i passaggi, o vero nel rimettere & rinforzar la voce quando bisogna: le quali cose, parte per arte, et parte per natura s'acquistano."

36. Cosimo Bartoli, *Ragionamenti accademici* (Venice, 1567), pp. 35–36: " . . . io so bene che Ocghem fu quasi il primo che in questi tempi, ritrovasse la Musica quasi che spenta del tutto: non altrimenti che Donatello ne suoi ritrovò la Scultura; et che Josquino discepolo di Ocghem si puo dire che quello alla Musica fusse un monstro della natura, si come è stato nella Architettura Pittura et Scultura il nostro Michielagnolo Buonarotti; perche si come Josquino

non hà però ancora havuto alcuno che lo arrivi nelle composizioni, cosi Michelagnolo ancora infrattuti coloro che in queste sue arti si sono esercitati, è solo et senza compagno; Et l'uno et l'altro di loro ha aperti gli occhi a tutti coloro che di queste arti si dilettano, o si diletteranno per lo avvenire."—Translation from Alfred Einstein, *The Italian Madrigal* (Princeton, N.J., 1949), I, 21.

37. See Edward E. Lowinsky, "The Concept of Physical and Musical Space in the Renaissance," pp. 66–74. *Idem,* "On the Use of Scores by Sixteenth-Century Musicians," *Journal of the American Musicological Society,* I (1948), 17–23, 20–21.

38. See Heinrich Besseler, *Bourdon und Fauxbourdon* (Leipzig, 1950), pp. 177 ff., in which Tinctoris' date is connected with Dufay's new *fauxbourdon* style of *ca.* 1430 in parallel sixth chords.

39. Couss. IV, 78a: "Hinc in primis animadvertendum sex tantum concordantiis, ut ex musica Boetii, ex dictisque Macrobii libro secundo in 'Summium [*sic*] Scipionis' accepi, nostros majores usos fuisse, id est diatessaron, diapenthe, diapason, diatessaron supra diapason, diapenthe super diapason ac bis diapason." Oddly enough, neither Boethius nor Macrobius had more than five consonances; both excluded the eleventh, i.e., the fourth plus octave, from the consonances. See *Boetii de institutione musica,* Bk. II, chap. xxvii: "Diatessaron ac diapason non esse secundum Pythagoricos consonantias"; see Bk. I, chap. VII, for the enumeration of the five consonances: fourth, fifth, octave, twelfth, double octave. For Macrobius, see *In somnium Scipionis,* Bk. II, chap. I: "Sunt igitur symphoniae quinque id est . . . ," and then follows the enumeration of Boethius' consonances in Greek.

Tinctoris has eight consonances in one octave and reaches the number of twenty-two by repeating them in a second and a third octave in their composite form, the third becoming a tenth and a seventeenth, etc. He denies that the composite forms are repetitions of the simple consonances: "Indeed," he exclaims, "I do not blush to assert that they really differ from their lower prototypes" ("immo eas differre realiter ab inferioribus asserere non erubesco") (Couss. IV, 79b), thereby again asserting the supremacy of the ear which certainly distinguishes between the sound of a third and that of a tenth.

40. *Tractatus de contrapuncto,* Couss. III, 193–99.

41. *Ibid.,* p. 195b: "et dicuntur imperfecte quia licet consonantiam bonam reddant auribus humanis, non tamen perfectam, sed imperfectam."

42. Couss. IV, 79a: "Perfectae sunt illae per quas tanquam principales et ad hoc magis aptas omnis cantus perfectiones constituuntur. . . . Imperfectae sunt per quas tanquam minus principales et ad hoc ineptas nulla cantus fit perfectio."

43. Couss. IV, 301b: " . . . separatis his [emended from "hic"] tribus perfectis consonantiis [fourth, fifth, octave], aliae sunt omnes dissonantiae, quamquam dytonus ac semidytonus, tonus cum dyapenthe sive semitonium, ac hujusmodi sint compassibiles. . . . "

44. Couss. IV, 325a, chap. xii: "Cur omnium dissonantiarum aliae sint auditui compassibiles, aliae vero non" (see chart, p. 327).

45. Couss. IV, 88a–b: "omnis sexta, sive perfecta sive imperfecta, sive

superior sive inferior fuerit, apud antiquos discordantia reputabatur, et ut vera fatear, aurium mearum judicio per se audita, hoc est sola, plus habet asperitatis quam dulcedinis . . . unde accuratissime notandum est nunquam sextam superiorem melodiose assumi posse, nisi eam una aut plures aliae sextae sequantur, finaliter ad octavam aut decimam superiorem sine interpositione concordantiae alterius speciei tendentes. . . . "

46. Couss. IV, 89a: "Nam semper et ubique sexta suavis est, si ei tertia vel decima supponatur, sed multo suavior si quinta vel duodecima . . . ," and then follows a three-part example illustrating the point.

47. According to Pythagorean theory, the third must be calculated by superpositions of four intervals of a fifth (2 : 3) minus two octaves (1 : 2). The formula is $(2/3)^4 : (1/2)^2 = 64/81$. It was the Englishman Odington writing *ca.* 1300 who suggested for the first time that $64 : 80 = (4 : 5)$ was so good an approximation of the Pythagorean formula that the interval of a major third as well as that of a minor third (5 : 6) might reasonably be regarded as consonances (see Hugo Riemann, *Geschichte der Musiktheorie*, [2nd ed.; Leipzig, 1920], pp. 119–20). This radical innovation of the medieval theory of consonances lay dormant until its revival by Bartolomeo Ramos (see following notes).

48. *Musica practica Bartolomei Rami de Pareia*, ed. J. Wolf (Leipzig, 1901), p. 98; translation in Strunk, *op. cit.*, p. 203.

49. *Le Istitutioni harmoniche* (Venice, 1558), Pt. 1, chap. viii: "Delle varie specie de Numeri" and the following chapters, in particular chap. xv: "Delle Proprietà del numero Senario, et delle sue parti; et come in esse si ritrova ogni consonanza musicale."

50. *Ibid.*, Proemio, pp. 1–2: "Nondimeno l'ottimo Iddio . . . ne hà conceduto gratia di far nascere a nostri tempi Adriano Willaert, veramente uno de più rari intelletti, che habbia la Musica prattica giamai essercitato: il quale a guisa di nuovo Pithagora essaminando minutamente quello, che in essa puote occorrere, et ritrovandovi infiniti errori, ha cominciato a levargli, et a ridurla verso quell' honore et dignità, che già ella era. . . . " ("Nonetheless, the good Lord has accorded us the grace to let be born, in our days, Adrian Willaert, truly one of the rarest intellects that ever cultivated the practice of music, who, a new Pythagoras, examining closely what she might lack, and finding there infinite errors, has begun to remove them, and to lead her back to that honor and dignity, that once was hers. . . . ")

51. Pt. 4, chap. xxxvi, p. 345: " . . . ne il Senso senza la ragione, ne la Ragione senza il senso potranno dare giuditio di qualunque oggetto scientifico: ma si bene quando queste due parti saranno aggiunte insieme."

52. *De institutione musica*, Bk. 1, chap. ix.

53. See pages 19, 21, 30, 38, 62, 96, 337. H. W. Janson, in his work on *Apes and Ape Lore in the Middle Ages and the Renaissance* (London, 1952), Appendix, "Titian's Laocoon Caricature and the Vesalian-Galenist Controversy," pp. 355–64, discusses and illustrates a precise parallel. In the second edition of his great work on anatomy, *De humani corporis fabrica libri VII*,

published in 1555, Vesalius uses a new and "specially cut initial V designed by an unknown artist, in which Apollo is shown preparing to flay Marsyas" (*ibid.*, p. 362). Having been attacked violently by the old guard of Galenists, led by his former teacher at the University of Paris, Jacobus Sylvius, Vesalius intimates, as Janson convincingly shows, that he, "the victorious 'Apollo,'" was now "about to 'dissect' his unsuccessful rival, the 'sylvan' Marsyas." That the Apollo-and-Marsyas motif fits better into the work of a musician than into that of an anatomist is obvious. The only question in our case is the identity of Marsyas: Is it the corporate body of medieval theory to be superseded by Zarlino's epoch-making new work? Is it perhaps Vicentino and the chromaticists (see above, p. 160–61)? And, final thought, does Apollo represent Zarlino, or possibly Willaert, who is credited in the Proemio with the revival of a decadent art? Or does he stand for Willaert-Zarlino, the unity of creator and thinker, master and disciple?

54. I have expressed my views on this problem in my articles, "The Concept of Physical and Musical Space in the Renaissance," pp. 72–74; "English Organ Music of the Renaissance," *Musical Quarterly*, XXXIX (1953), 541 n.; "Music in the Culture of the Renaissance," *Journal of the History of Ideas*, XV (1954), 529–35.

55. *De arte poetica*, 355. The English version is from *Horace: Satires, Epistles, Ars Poetica*, trans. H. Rushton Fairclough (London and New York, 1926), p. 479.

56. The reference is probably to Cicero's *De oratore*, Bk. ii, chap. lxxxii, para. 334: "Contio capit omnem vim orationis et gravitatem varietatemque desiderat."

57. Tinctoris refers apparently to *Nichomachean Ethics*, Bk. viii, chap. xiv (see *The Basic Works of Aristotle*, ed. Richard McKeon [New York, 1941], p. 1058): "There is no one thing that is always pleasant, because our nature is not simple. . . . This is why God always enjoys a single and simple pleasure; for there is not only an activity of movement but an activity of immobility, and pleasure is found more in rest than in movement. But 'change in all things is sweet', as the poet says. . . . "

58. Couss. IV, 152*a–b*: "Octava si quidem et ultima regula haec est quod in omni contrapuncto varietas accuratissime exquirenda est, nam ut HORATIUS in sua poetica dicit: Cytharedus ridetur corda si semper oberrat eadem. Quemadmodum enim in arte dicendi varietas secundum TULLII sententiam, auditorem maxime delectat, ita et in musica concentuum diversitas animam auditorum vehementer in oblectamentum provocat, hinc et philosophus, in Ethicis, varietatem jocundissimam rem esse naturamque humanam ejus indigentem asserere non dubitavit."

59. *Ibid.*, 152*b*: "Verumtamen in his omnibus summa est adhibenda ratio . . . nec tot nec tales varietates uni cantilenae congruunt quot et quales uni moteto, nec tot et tales [Coussemaker has *quales*] uni moteto quot et quales uni missae."

60. The first music theorist of the Renaissance who had Greek treatises

translated into Latin for his own use seems to have been Gafori (see P. O. Kristeller, "Music and Learning in the Early Italian Renaissance," p. 268). The first one to have mastered Greek appears to have been Glareanus, whose main profession, of course, was that of a humanist and a professor of rhetoric. He was so proud of his superiority over other writers on music in this respect that he wrote, playing on the old antithesis between *musicus* and *cantor*: "How is it that there are so few musicians nowadays, and such a big crowd of singers? Unquestionably, because so few know Greek!"—*Isagoge in musicen* (Basel, 1516), chap. i.

61. Couss. IV, 154*a*: "Tamen qualiter pronunciaverint aut composuerint scripto nobis minime constat, verum elegantissime id eos fecisse verisimilimum est."

62. One notable exception is D. P. Walker who, in his "Musical Humanism in the Sixteenth and Early Seventeenth Centuries," *Music Review,* II (1941), and III (1943) (available also in German translation, *Der musikalische Humanismus im 16. und frühen 17. Jahrhundert* [Kassel, 1949]), concentrated on the "effects," and in particular on their ethical side. It is a most useful study, even though "the author is disposed to underestimate the contribution made by fifteenth- and early sixteenth-century theory to the revival of ancient musical thought and literature" (see my review in *Musical Quarterly,* XXXVII [April, 1951], 285–89). See also Frances A. Yates, *The French Academies of the Sixteenth Century* (London, 1949), in particular chap. iii.

63. Couss. IV, 191–200.

64. Couss. IV, 200*b*: "Hos igitur effectus, si quis advertat, nunquam ei pigebit ingenium suum huic parti discipline applicuisse: imo in dies affectu flagrantissimo melodie studebit, qua reges, qua ceteros principes, quaque liberos homines usos fuisse et uti, gloriosum et commendabile est. Hec enim est que a Lycurgo, Platone, Quintiliano approbatur precipiturque, quorum precepta qui sequitur, et ars illi, et ille arti decori in sempiternum erit."

65. *Franchini Gafuri Theorica musicae* (facs. ed.; Rome, 1934), with a Preface by Gaetano Cesari. The opening chapter is entitled: "De musicis et effectibus atque comendatione musice discipline capitulum primum."

66. In his treatise on *Complexus effectuum musices* (Couss. IV, 193), Tinctoris reports about the use of music in the divine rites of ancient Rome, and adds: "Sed haec ad falsam religionem pertinent." He goes on to speak of King David as "verae religionis cultor." Most likely, Tinctoris made implied reference to the book *De falsa religione* by Lactantius, the early Christian writer, still quoted by Zarlino as attributing the invention of the lyre to Apollo (*Istitutioni,* p. 3).

67. *Musica practica Bartolomei Rami de Pareia,* ed. J. Wolf (Leipzig, 1901), p. 2: "Quaelibet fabulosa et fidem excedentia videantur, mirabilium tamen operum effectricem esse musicam non dubium est."

68. "Hi fuere, quos venerabilis antiquitas adeo mirata est, ut eos dixerit carminis dulcedine movisse feras, corda hominum possedisse, animas in corpora revocasse, manes ad misericordiam inflexisse et duras traxisse e montibus ornos."—*Ibid.*

69. "Quodsi hac nostra tempestate tot miracula per musicam minime fiant, non arti, quae supra naturam perfectissima est, sed arte male utentibus imputandum est. Si enim illi, quorum supra meminimus, probatissimi musici ad vitam revocarentur, musicam nostri temporis a se inventam negarent: usque adeo inepta, inconcinna dissipataque quorundam cantorum depravatione reddita est."—*Ibid.*, p. 3.

70. For literature consult works cited in note 62.

71. See James Hutton, "Some English Poems in Praise of Music," *English Miscellany*, II (1951), 1–63. For a broad treatment of "Ideas of Music in English Poetry, 1500–1700," see John Hollander, *The Untuning of the Sky* (Princeton, N.J., 1961).

72. Ambros, usually so perceptive, questions the soundness of mind of the late Renaissance writers such as Galilei and Doni, who in their "blind" respect for the Greeks believed in the "miracles of ancient music" (see *Geschichte der Musik* [Leipzig, 1881], IV, 155–56; cf. D. P. Walker, *op. cit.*, p. 13, n. 39).

73. We can observe the transformation of music as handmaid of theology to an art ministering to human needs in Tinctoris' treatise on the effects of music (Couss. IV, 191–200). The first six effects are these: "music pleases God; music enhances the praise of God; music augments the joys of the Blessed; music assimilates the militant to the triumphant Church; music prepares for the reception of God's benediction; music stirs souls to piety." Theological overtones vibrate even in the series of psychological effects now following: "music expels melancholy; it resolves stubbornness of heart; it drives the devil away [he refers here to the story of David's playing the harp for the disturbed Saul]; it causes ecstasy; it elevates the earthly mind; it changes bad intention; it gladdens the human heart; it heals the sick, tempers the strains of toil, incites the soul to battle, it lures it to love, it adds to convivial gaiety," and—pride of the Renaissance musician—"renders famous those who cultivate it." Finally, "it sanctifies the soul."

74. On Orpheus as a symbol of the power of music, see F. A. Yates, *The French Academies*, Index; on Orpheus in English literature, see John Hollander, *The Untuning of the Sky*, Index. In the immense literature of dedications, prefaces, and dedicatory or introductory poems to musical publications of the Renaissance, Orpheus is an almost omnipresent figure.

75. On the Timotheus tradition from antiquity through the Renaissance, see Erwin Panofsky, *Early Netherlandish Painting* (Cambridge, Mass., 1953), Vol. I, n. 1972; see also the same author's article "Who is Jan van Eyck's 'Tymotheos'?", *Journal of the Warburg and Courtauld Institutes*, XII (1949), pp. 80 ff., in which he formulated for the first time the brilliant hypothesis that Jan van Eyck's portrait inscribed "Tymotheos" presents Gilles Binchois. See further Nan Carpenter, "Spenser and Timotheus: A Musical Gloss on E. K.'s Gloss," *PMLA*, LXXI, No. 5 (1956), 1141–51.

76. See note 78 for a clear enunciation of the idea of expression as opposed to contrapuntal and mensural complexity.

77. On these changes and their significance, see Edward E. Lowinsky, "The Concept of Physical and Musical Space in the Renaissance," pp. 57–84,

particularly 66–75; *idem*, "Music in the Culture of the Renaissance," *Journal of the History of Ideas*, XV, No. 4 (1954), 509–53, especially 528–43. I should like to refer here to Professor Janson's brilliant paper on "The Image of Man in Renaissance Art: Donatello to Michelangelo," in this volume. His demonstration of the Renaissance revival of the free-standing statue, i.e., the human figure freed from the domination of an architectural ensemble, seems to me the sculptor's equivalent of the composer's emancipation of polyphony from *cantus firmus* technique. In both cases this means also a liberation from an ensemble of theological-allegorical ideas.

78. My translation. See the facsimile edition by Manfred Bukofzer, *Documenta musicologica*, (Kasel, 1954), Vol. IX, F2: " . . . ne inhaereant prolixis scriptis Musicorum Mathematicorum, qui finxerunt tot signorum augmentationis et diminutionis genera, ex quibus nullus fructus, litis vero et discordiae plurimum oritur, ac res per se quidem clara difficillima redditur: Verum omnes animi vires adhibeant, ut ornate canant, et textum suo loco applicent, quia Musica à Deo condita est ad suaviter modulandum, non ad rixandum, ac vere Musicus est et habetur, non qui de numeris, prolationibus, signis ac valoribus multa novit garrire et scribere, sed qui doctè et dulciter canit, cuilibet notae debitam syllabam applicans, ac ita componit ut laetis verbis laetos addat numeros et econtra etc."

79. On the change in the text repertory of the motet, see E. Lowinsky, *Das Antwerpener Motettenbuch Orlando di Lassos* (The Hague, 1937), especially pp. 77–78; on the Dido lament in Renaissance polyphony, see Oliver Strunk, "Vergil in Music," *Musical Quarterly*, XVI, No. 4 (1930), 482–97, especially 485–90; and Helmut Osthoff, "Vergils Aeneis in der Musik von Josquin des Prez bis Orlando di Lasso," *Archiv für Musikwissenschaft*, XI, No. 2 (1953), 85–102.

80. Bk. iii, chap. xxiv; translation by Oliver Strunk, *Source Readings*, pp. 220–21.

81. *Ibid.*, pp. 226–27.

82. While in general the development of polyphony in the sixteenth century goes in the direction of a decrease in contrapuntal complexity and an increase in expressive design, counterpoint and expression are by no means mutually exclusive. Josquin was perfectly capable of writing an expressive counterpoint over a given *cantus firmus* or even over a canon. The latter he does with supreme skill in his chansons, the former in such famous works as his *Miserere*, his *Déploration* on the death of Ockeghem, or his passion motet *Huc me sydereo*. It is with regard to the last named that Johannes Otto in the preface to the *Secundus tomus novi operis musici* (1538) exclaims: "What painter could render Christ's face in the agony of death as graphically as did Josquin in tones?" (For the original text, see my study on "Music in the Culture of the Renaissance," p. 524, in which I connected this remark, erroneously, with the passion motet cited in the following footnote.)

83. The greatest work in this genre is perhaps Josquin's *O Domine Jesu Christe*, written for four voices in five *partes* (*Werken van Josquin Des Prés*, ed. A. Smijers, Motetten, Bundel II [Amsterdam and Leipzig, 1925], pp. 35–47).

84. In his denunciation of Guido of Arezzo, Ramos had a predecessor in

the fourteenth-century innovator Marchettus of Padua. Ramos' sarcastic commentary might well have been inspired by Gallicus' spirited defense of the venerable Aretinian against Marchettus as not only an experienced musician, but "pium monachum ac in ecclesia Dei famosissimum suo tempore."—Couss. IV, 324*a*.

85. Gallicus preceded Ramos in the vigorous condemnation of the complexities of the system of mutations while trying to absolve Guido from the burden of responsibility for these "frivolous" inventions (Couss. IV, 374*b*). This is surely the chief reason why Ramos praised a man whose views on music were otherwise diametrically opposed to his own in these words (*Musica practica*, ed. J. Wolf, p. 44): "Well said that Brother Johannes the Carthusian: 'I speak not of a mutation of one syllable to another, but of a variation of one circumlocution to another. All that is needed is to note tones and semitones and sing with Gregory's [alphabetical] letters.' The same do I say about my syllables." In the concluding statement, Ramos is referring to the eight new syllables given by him to the eight notes—an invention designed to do away with the three hexachords, the thirty-six mutations, and the distinctions between an *ordo naturalis* and an *ordo accidentalis*. Ramos was centuries ahead of his time: the complexities of the medieval system survived in teaching methods into the eighteenth century, when the old controversy flared up for the last time in the famous encounter between Butstett and Mattheson (see Blume's excellent account in *Musik in Geschichte und Gegenwart*, II, cols. 533–40).

86. I refer here to a passage unnoticed, I believe, in discussions of equal temperament. Ramos (*op. cit.*, p. 50) mentions the traditional division of the octave into a fifth and a fourth, and then goes on, counter to all medieval tradition, to propose a division of the octave into an "almost equal quantity," namely, tritone and diminished fifth, "for the distance between B and F is the same as that between F and B, what difference there is does not matter to the practical musician, it does, however, to the theoretician who speculates on the difference of the semitone," that is, between the major and minor semitone. ("Est tamen alia quantitas, quae quasi nihil differt in sono, in quam diapason dividi potest, utputa tritonus et diapente imperfecta, quae vocatur semidiapente, ut b f et f ♮ , quoniam tanta distantia est inter b f, quanta inter f ♮ nec differt practicorum differentia, secus tamen theoricorum, qui differentiam semitonii speculantur.") The traditional medieval view is expressed by Jacobus of Liége, already noted earlier for his anti-Aristoxenian position. In the second book of his *Speculum musicae* (chap. xcvii, pp. 224–38, esp. 226–27), he argues against the famous Aristoxenian theorem that the octave consists of six equal whole tones. If this were true, Jacobus observes, one could divide the octave into two equal halves, two tritones. The interval thus achieved, however, would not be an octave, but a "hexatone." The intervals of the hexatone would be "rudae et dissonae." Here is a case, he says, in which, according to Ptolemy, Aristoxenus' error becomes perceptible to the senses, not only understandable on mathematical grounds—a position precisely negated by Ramos.

87. *Op. cit.*, p. 103: "Pugnam non timeo, si praesente et iudicante ratione pugnabitur."

88. *Ibid.*, p. 42: "Sed non miror, quia sequax Guidonis est. Ego enim

caput conterere volo, ut corpus istud in erroribus constitutum cadaver iam fiat nec amplius vivere possit."

89. *Ibid.*, p. 81: "Nam defectus est in matheseos disciplinis per comparationem aliqua probare."

90. "Nicolai Burtii Parmensis, musices professoris ac iuris pontificii studiosissimi, musices opusculum incipit cum defensione Guidonis Aretini adversus quendam Hispanum veritatis praevaricatorem."—Fragments published by J. Wolf in his edition of the Ramos treatise, pp. 105–9.

91. See P. O. Kristeller, "Music and Learning," p. 267.

92. Burtius, *Musices opusculum*, chap. xii (not published by Wolf).

93. At one point he speaks of "divina inspirante gratia," at another, of "divino quodam nutu" (*ibid.*, chap. xiii).

94. See J. Wolf's edition (*op. cit.*, pp. 109–12) for excerpts from the writings of Hothby and Gafori directed against Ramos.

95. *Ibid.*, p. 45: " . . . ut non solum sit utilis ecclesiastico cantui, verum etiam seculari curiosiori."

96. *Ibid.*: "Erit igitur musica Gregorii, Ambrosii, Augustini, Bernardi, Isidori, Oddonis enchiridion, Guidonis, qui ab istis quasi totam assumpsit"—an additional slur on Guido—"suorumque sequentium sicut lex scripturae, quae non omnibus data fuit; nam aliqui sine ea hodierna die cantant. Nostra autem catholica sive universalis erit sicut lex gratiae, quae legem scripturae in se continet atque naturae. Sic etiam nostra totum, quod isti ecclesiastici viri et sapientissimi musici antiqui dixerunt et invenerunt, continebit."

97. *Ibid.*, pp. 106–7: "Postmodum si Gregorius illis tantum septem voluerit uti latinis litteris quotiens opus fuerit replicatis et Ambrosius atque Augustinus vestigia haec maluerint imitari quam aliena, cur non erubescis hunc ordinem pervertere et tuo supercilio censorio depravare? Tu sanctior forsan elegantiorque his columnis ecclesiae aut peritior? . . . Nam pii monachi doctrina, quae per universum sparsa, tum et ecclesiae approbatione, tum et notularum inventione mirabili in aevum tuo non obstante livore est duratura."

98. I refer in particular to the Spataro correspondence (see Edward E. Lowinsky, "Adrian Willaert's 'Chromatic Duo' Re-examined," *Tijdschrift voor Muziekwetenschap*, XVIII, [1956], 1–36, especially 5–28).

99. Willaert's chromatic experiment stands isolated in his own *oeuvre*, and it took a generation until similar experiments were published (see Edward E. Lowinsky, "Matthaeus Greiter's *Fortuna*: An Experiment in Chromaticism and in Musical Iconography," *Musical Quarterly*, Vol. XLII, No. 4 (1956), and Vol. XLIII, No. 1 (1957). Compositions by Ramos (*Tu lumen*) and by Spataro (a motet in honor of Leo X), which are probably the first polyphonic works in which the Greek genders were used, have been lost.

100. See the facsimile edition by Edward E. Lowinsky, *Documenta musicologica*, Vol. XVII (Kassel, 1959).

101. *L'Antica musica*, Bk. 1, chap. xxxv: " . . . é molto necessario quando aviene che nelle parole si vuol dimostrare un effetto maraviglioso."

102. For a discussion of Zarlino's aesthetics of expression, see Edward E. Lowinsky, "Music in the Culture of the Renaissance," pp. 536–38.

103. Letter of September 26, 1781, *Mozarts Briefe und Aufzeichnungen,* ed. W. A. Bauer and O. E. Deutsch, 4 vols. (Kassel, 1962–63), III, 162.

104. See chap. lxxx of the third part entitled "Opinioni delli Chromatisti ributtate," *op. cit.*, pp. 290–92. Although Vicentino is not mentioned by name, he was the obvious butt of Zarlino's remarks, being then the only one among the *chromatisti* who had ventured to have his ideas on the new musical gospel published. The opinions opposed are demonstrably those uttered by him.

105. This comparison was suggested, years ago, by Professor Millard Meiss when I read a paper on "The Concept of Music in the Renaissance" to the University Seminar on the Renaissance at Columbia University under the chairmanship of Professor Hermann Randall, Jr. Professor Meiss suggested that Tinctoris might well have read Alberti's treatise—a supposition borne out, I believe, by the comparison following.

106. See Leon Battista Alberti, *On Painting,* trans. John R. Spencer (New Haven, Conn., 1956), p. 43.

107. *The Codex Huygens and Leonardo da Vinci's Art Theory* (London, 1940), p. 97; see on harmony and perspective, E. E. Lowinsky, "The Concept of Physical and Musical Space in the Renaissance," pp. 81–82,

108. John White, *The Birth and Rebirth of Pictorial Space* (New York, 1958), p. 122.

109. *On Painting*, p. 63.

110. *Ibid.*, p. 75.

111. *Ibid.*, p. 80.

112. *Ibid.*, p. 77: " . . . be careful not to repeat the same gesture or pose."

113. This forms the sixth rule of counterpoint in Tinctoris' treatise in which he admonishes composers and improvising singers to avoid repetition of musical figures ("redictas evitare"); see Couss. IV, pp. 150–51.

114. *Op. cit.*, p. 79.

115. Erwin Panofsky, "The History of the Theory of Human Proportions as a Reflection of the History of Styles," in *Meaning in the Visual Arts* (New York, 1955), pp. 55–107, 91.

116. *Ibid.*, p. 98.

117. See my study on "The Concept of Physical and Musical Space in the Renaissance," pp. 66–70.

118. See Edward E. Lowinsky, *Tonality and Atonality in Sixteenth-Century Music* (Berkeley, Calif., 1961), especially chaps. i, ii, v, vi.

NOTES ON THE CONTRIBUTORS

DOUGLAS BUSH, Gurney Professor of English Literature at Harvard University, graduated in Classics at the University of Toronto. He has received honorary degrees from Tufts, Princeton, Toronto, Oberlin, Harvard, Swarthmore, Southern Illinois, and Boston College. He was president of the Modern Humanities Research Association in 1955, is a member of the American Philosophical Society, and a Corresponding Fellow of the British Academy. Among his books are *English Literature in the Earlier Seventeenth Century* (Oxford History of English Literature), *Mythology and the Renaissance Tradition in English Poetry, The Renaissance and English Humanism, Paradise Lost in Our Time,* and *Prefaces to Renaissance Literature.*

HORST W. JANSON, professor of fine arts at New York University, has also taught at the University of Iowa and at Washington University. The author of articles on medieval and Renaissance art, he has most recently concentrated his studies on Donatello and his followers. His book *The Sculpture of Donatello* contains an authoritative catalogue of Donatello's works and provides a new assessment of this sculptor's importance as a creator of the Renaissance. Co-author with his wife of *The Story of Painting for Young People* and *History of Art,* Professor Janson, who has twice been a Guggenheim fellow, is affiliated with the Institute of Fine Arts at New York University.

PAUL OSKAR KRISTELLER, professor of philosophy at Columbia University, received his Ph.D. degree from the University of Heidelberg, and has taught at the Istituto Superiore di Magistero in Florence, at the University of Pisa, and at Yale University. He has lectured at many universities in the United States and abroad. Among his books and articles are *The Philosophy of Marsilio Ficino, The Classics and Renaissance Thought,* and *Studies in Renaissance Thought and Letters.* He is a member of numerous learned societies and editorial boards in this country and in Europe, and has received the Serena Medal of the British Academy for his work in Italian studies.

EDWARD E. LOWINSKY, Ferdinand Schevill Distinguished Service Professor at the University of Chicago, teaches musicology in the Department of Music. At the University of Heidelberg, where he received his Ph.D. degree in musicology, he also studied philosophy and art history. From 1933 to 1939, he lived and taught privately in Holland. Since moving to the United States, he has taught at Black Mountain College, Queens College, and the University of California, Berkeley. The recipient of grants from the Guggenheim Foundation, the Institute for Advanced Study at Princeton, and the Bollingen Foundation, he is the author of *Orlando di Lassos Antwerpener Motetten-buch, Secret Chromatic Art in the Netherlands Motet, Tonality and Atonality in Sixteenth Century Music,* and numerous essays in musical periodicals here and abroad. He is also General Editor of *Monuments of Renaissance Music,* published by the University of Chicago Press.

BERNARD O'KELLY, assistant professor of English at the Ohio State University, is editor of *John Colet's Commentary on I Corinthians,* to be published shortly by the Clarendon Press. He is editor of Thomas More's *Answer to a Poisoned Book* in the Yale Edition of the Works of St. Thomas More, and was chairman of the Fourth Annual Conference on the Humanities, "The Renaissance Image of Man and the World," sponsored by the Ohio State University Graduate School in October, 1961.

GIORGIO DE SANTILLANA, professor of the history and philosophy of science at the Massachusetts Institute of Technology, has taught physics at the University of Milan, has helped to organize the School for the History of Science at the University of Rome, has lectured at the Sorbonne, and has conducted colloquia at Brussels and Pontigny. Since coming to the United States, he has lectured at many universities. He is the recipient of a Fullbright professorship, a Guggenheim fellowship, and a National Science Foundation fellowship, and is a member of the American Academy of Arts and Sciences, the History of Science Society, the Examiner Club, l'Académie Internationale d'Histoire des Sciences, and is a Knight Commander of the Order of Merit of Italy. He is the author of *Galileo's Dialogue on the Great World Systems, The Crime of Galileo, The Age of Adventure,* and *The Origins of Scientific Thought.*

INDEX

Abano, Pietro d', 123

Abu Ezra, 123

Abu Mashar, 119–21, 123

Achilles, 63

Actaeon, 47

Aeneas Sylvius de Piccolomini (Pope Pius II), 114

Africa, 60; *see also* Petrarch

Al Battani, 120

Alberti, Leone Battista, 33, 42, 43, 83, 95, 97, 99–100, 108–9, 113, 127, 161–63; *see also Della pittura; De statua; Intercænales*

Albumasar; *see* Abu Mashar

Alciati, Andrea, 60

Alciato, Andrea, 33

Alexander, 152

Al-Kalisi, 123

Ambros, August Wilhelm, 151, 158

Anatomy of Melancholy, 74

Andrea da Firenze, 84

"Angel with Tambourine," 95–96, Plate XIV

Antica musica ridotta alla moderna prattica, L'; see Vicentino, Nicola

"Antinous, Head of," *see* "Head of Antinous"

Apollo, 147–48, 172 n. 66

Aquinas; *see* St. Thomas Aquinas

Aragazzi, Bartolommeo, 98

Archimides, 111, 112

Ariosto, Ludovico, 54, 60, 67, 68

Aristophanes, 67

Aristotelianism (–ists), 34–35, 37, 38, 40, 43, 46, 68; *see also* Aristotle

Aristotle, 33, 34, 37, 39, 40, 43, 65, 67, 68, 71, 115, 131, 149, 150; *see also* Aristotelianism (–ists), *Ethics, Metaphysics, Poetics, Rhetoric*

Aristoxenus, 137–38, 146–47, 175 n. 86

Arnobius, 80

Arnold, Matthew, 62

Aron, Pietro, 130

Arte of Rhetorique (Thomas Wilson), 59

Ascham, Roger, 17–18, 62

Ascoli, Cecco d', 123, 124

"Assumption of the Virgin" (Nanni di Banco), 90

Averroism, 37

Bacon, Francis, 40, 55, 57, 60, 61, 64, 70
Barbaro, Ermolao, 35
Bartoli, Cosimo, 141
"Bearded prophet" (Donatello), 91, Plate VI
"Beardless prophet" (Donatello), 91, Plate VI, Plate IX
Beatrice of Aragon, 150, 166 n. 15
Bembo, Pietro, 22, 60, 66
Bernelinus, *see* Pseudo-Bernelinus
Binchois, Gilles, 133, 173 n. 75
Biondo, Flavio, 58
Bisticci, Vespasiano da, 98
Boccaccio, Giovanni, 68, 70
Boethius, 135, 137, 138, 139, 143, 147, 167 n. 27, 168 n. 33
Boke Named the Governor, The; see Elyot, Sir Thomas
Bonatti, Guido, 123
Bono, Pietro, 140
Book of Common Prayer, 64
Botticelli, Sandro, 122
Brahe, Tycho, 120
Brandes, George, 65, 126
Browne, Sir Thomas, 61
Brunelleschi, Filippo, 79, 82–83, 96, 107–8, 109, 110–12, 113, 127, 162
Bruni, Leonardo, 42, 43, 45, 58, 77, 79, 87, 92, 97; tomb of, 97–100
Bruno, Giordano, 40, 47, 114, 124
Buchanan, George, 60
Burckhardt, Jacob, 53
Burdach, Konrad, 37
Burtius, Nicolaus, 158, 159
Burton, Robert, 61; *see also Anatomy of Melancholy*
Busnois, Antoine, 133, 139

Calvin, John, 73
Camoens, Luis de; *see Lusiad*
Cardan, Jerome, 123, 125
Caron, Firmin (or Philippe), 133
Castiglione, Baldassare, 22, 56, 57, 60, 63
Caxton, William, 20

Celoria, 126
Cervantes Saavedra, Miguel de, 54, 71, 75; *see also* Shelton, Thomas
Chapman, George, 62, 63, 70, 73
Chaucer, Geoffrey, 20, 21–23, 24, 66
Chellini, Giovanni, 101 n. 13
Cherichini, Giovanni di Barduccio, 93
Cicero, 42, 59, 61, 71, 149, 150, 171 n. 56; *see also* Ciceronianism
Ciceronianism, 56, 58, 61, 64
Ciceronianus; see Erasmus, Desiderius
Coclico, Adrian Petit, 130, 153–54
Colet, John, 21, 55, 56
Columbus, Christopher, 19, 117, 118–19, 122, 123
Comes, Natalis, 70
Comparetti, Domenico, 120
Compendium Musices; see Coclico, Adrian Petit
Complexus effectuum musices; see Tinctoris, Johannes
Copernicus, 110, 111, 113
Courtier, The, 56, 63
Crashaw, Richard, 60
Cujas, Jacques de, 33
Cusanus; *see* Nicholas of Cusa

D'Ailly, Pierre, 118, 119
Daniel, Samuel, 5, 72–73
Dante Alighieri, 111, 124
"David" (Gaddi), 85, Plate III
"David," by Donatello (bronze), 83–84, 94–96, 97, Plates I, XII
"David," by Donatello (marble), 84–88, 93, 94, 96, 97, Plate II
"David," by Michelangelo, 90, 96–97, Plate IV
"David," by Michelangelo (drawing), 96, Plate XIV
De arte contrapuncti (Tinctoris), 132–33
De arte poetica, 148, 149
Della pittura (Alberti), 161–63
Democritus, 46
Dentice, Luigi, 140–41

De Oratore (Cicero), 149
Deschamps, Eustache, 22
De statua (Alberti), 83–84
Dialoghi; see Dentice, Luigi
Dodekachordon; see Glareanus,
    Henricus
Don Quixote; see Cervantes Saavedra,
    Miguel de; Shelton, Thomas
Donatello, 77–100 *passim; see also*
    separate works
Doni, Giovanni Battista, 173 n. 72
Donne, John, 66, 75
"Dovizia," 93–94
Du Bartas, Guillaume de Saluste, 62
Dufay, Guillaume, 133, 142
Dunn, Charles W., 22
Dunstable, John, 23, 133

"E.K.," 66; *see also* Spenser, Edmund
Eliot, T. S., 74
Elyot, Sir Thomas, 56, 74
Erasmus, Desiderius, 11, 21, 33, 55,
    56, 61, 70–71, 105, 113; works of:
    Ciceronianus, 61; *The Praise of
    Folly,* 61
Eroici Furori; see Bruno, Giordano
Este, Yppolito d', 160
Ethics (Aristotle), 149

Faerie Queene, The, 9, 66–67
Feltre, Vittorino da, 71, 134, 135
Ficino, Marsilio, 37, 39, 42–47 *passim,*
    70, 116, 117, 123
Florio, John, 62
"Four Saints" (Nanni di Banco);
    see "Quattro Coronati"

Gaddi, Taddeo, 85
Gafori, Franchino, 130, 150–51, 158,
    168 n. 30, 171 n. 60
Galilei, Galileo, 40, 107, 108, 109, 113
Galilei, Vincenzo, 130, 173 n. 72
Gallicus, Johannes, 133–35, 144–45,
    150, 154, 175 n. 85

Garin, Eugenio, 106–7
Gascoigne, George, 3, 7, 17, 25–26
Ghiberti, Lorenzo, 85, 103 n. 27, 108
Glareanus, Henricus, 155–56,
    172 n. 60
Golden Bough, The, 70
Golding, Arthur, 63
Gosson, Stephen, 18
Governor [*The Boke Named the*];
    see Elyot, Sir Thomas
Great Conjunctions, The; see
    Abu Mashar
Gregorian chant, 133–35, 144
Gregory I, Pope, 135, 159
Greville, Fulke, 73
Griglio, Giovanni, 102 n. 14
Grotius, Hugo, 60
Guido of Arezzo, 139, 140, 147, 151,
    157, 158, 159, 168 n. 33

Harington, Sir John, 68
Hartner, Willy, 119–20
Harvey, Gabriel, 66
"Head of Antinous," 95, Plate XIII
*History of Magic and Experimental
    Science; see* Thorndike, Lynn
Hoby, Sir Thomas, 63
Holland, Philemon, 62
Homer, 62, 63, 67
Hooker, Richard, 64, 72, 74
Horace, 65, 67, 148–49, 150
Hothby, John, 157, 158

Intercænales, 113
Introductorium (Abu Mashar), 119
"Isaiah" (Nanni di Banco), 84–86,
    88, Plate II
Jacobus of Liége, 165 n. 5, 167 n. 24,
    175 n. 86
"Jeremiah" (Donatello), 92–93,
    Plates VII, XI
Jerusalem Delivered, 67; *see also*
    Tasso, Torquato
Joachim of Fiora, 122
John of Garland, 119, 120

Jonson, Ben, 59, 65, 70, 73
"Joshua" (Donatello), 89, 96, 97, 101 n. 14
Josquin des Prez, 141, 154–56, 164

Kepler, Johann, 113, 114, 120, 124, 127
Kircher, Athanasius, 123
Krautheimer, Richard, 109
Kugler, K. X., 121

Landino, Cristoforo, 43, 125
Lanfranc, 37
Laudatio Florentinae Urbis, 77
Leibniz, Gottfried Wilhelm, 114
Leonardo da Vinci, 57, 111, 113, 122, 125, 150
Le Roy, Louis, 58
Levin, Harry, 74
Lusiad, The (Luis de Camoens), 67
Luther, Martin, 71, 73
Lysippus, 81; *see also* "Venus," Lysippean

Machaut, Guillaume de, 142
Machiavelli, Niccolò, 37, 38, 54, 57
Macrobius, 169 n. 39
Manetti, Giannozzo, 108
Mantuan, 60
Marchettus of Padua, 165 n. 5, 174 n. 84
Marlowe, Christopher, 20
Maro, Virgilius; *see* Virgil
Marsuppini, Carlo, 98–99
Marsyas, 147–48
Martin, Fernam, 117, 122
Masaccio, 79, 83, 108
Medici, Cosimo de', 93, 107
Medici, Lorenzo de', 117
Medici, The, 77, 93, 96
Mei, Girolamo, 164 n. 2
Meiss, Millard, 177 n. 105
Melanchthon, Philip, 33, 112
Metamorphoses (Ovid), 63

Metaphysics (Aristotle), 33
Michelangelo, 77, 96–97, 141, 164; *see also* separate works
Milton, John, 55, 56, 59, 60, 70, 71
Montaigne, Michel de, 38, 41, 42, 55, 57, 62, 72–73, 74, 75, 105; *see also* Florio, John
Monteverdi, Claudio, 130
More, Sir Thomas, 55, 60, 122
Mozart, Wolgang Amadeus, 161

Nanni di Banco, 84–86; 88, 90; *see also* separate works
Nativity; see Milton, John
Neoplatonism, 112, 123; *see also* Plotinus
Newton, Isaac, 127
Niccoli, Niccolò, 107
Nicholas V, Pope, 31
Nicholas of Cusa, 34, 39, 113–16, 118
North, Sir Thomas, 62, 64
Novum Organum; see Bacon, Francis

Ockhamism, 37
Ockeghem, Johannes, 133, 139, 141
Odington, Walter, 170 n. 47
Odyssey; see Chapman, George; Homer
Of Education; see Milton, John
Orbus, 140
Orlando Furioso; see Ariosto, Ludovico
Orpheus, 152
Orwell, George, 62
Otto, Johannes, 174 n. 82
Ovid, 22, 62, 63, 67, 69, 149, 150; *see also* Golding, Arthur
Owen, John, 60

Palmieri, Matteo, 42
Pantheon, 99–100
Patrizi, Francesco, 40
Paul the physician; *see* Toscanelli, Paolo
Pedro, Prince of Portugal, 112

Pelagius, 71

Petrarch, 22, 30, 41, 43, 58, 60, 162

Pico della Mirandola, Giovanni, 35, 39, 42, 74, 119, 122, 123

Pippo, Maestro; *see* Brunelleschi, Filippo

Pisano, Giovanni, 82, 84, 94, Plate I; *see also* "Venus"; "Virtue"

Pius II, Pope; *see* Aeneas Sylvius

Plato, 12, 40, 67, 71, 72, 115, 123, 126, 150; *see also* Platonism

Platonism, 18, 37, 38–39, 43, 45, 47, 56, 68, 70

Pléiade, The, 66; *see also* Ronsard, Pierre de

Pliny the Elder, 81, 118

Plotinus, 46; *see also* Neoplatonism

Plutarch, 57, 62, 67; *see also* North, Sir Thomas

Poetics (Aristotle), 68

Poggio Bracciolini, Gian Francesco, 98, 107

Poliziano, Angelo, 60

Pomponazzi, Pietro, 34, 42, 43, 44, 46–47

Pontano, Giovanni, 60

Praise of Folly, The; see Erasmus

Proemio, 147–48; *see also* Zarlino, Gioseffo, da Chioza

Proportionale (Tinctoris), 149–50

Prosdocimo de Beldemandis, 143, 165 n. 10

Pseudo-Bernelinus, 138

Pythagoras, 39, 137-38; *see also* Pythagoreanism

Pythagoreanism, 110, 115, 125, 131, 137–38, 144, 145–47, 164

"Quattro Coronati" (Nanni di Banco), 88–89

Quintilian, 150

Rabelais, François, 54, 55, 62, 75; *see also* Urquhart, Sir Thomas

Ragionomenti accademici; see Bartoli, Cosimo

Ralegh, Sir Walter, 3, 67, 73

Ramos, Bartolomeo, 144, 147, 151, 152, 157–60

Regiomontanus, 111, 116, 126

Regis, Johannes, 133

Renaissance Studies; see Garin, Eugenio

Rhetoric (Aristotle), 34

Richard III, King, 19, 20

Riemzo, Cola di, 37

Robbia, Luca della, 108

Ronsard, Pierre de, 64–65

Rossellino, Bernardo, 97–100

St. Ambrose, 37, 159

St. Augustine, 37, 46, 71, 150, 159, 168 n. 31

"St. Christopher"; *see* Griglio, Giovani

"St. George" (Donatello), 89–90, 97, Plate IV

"St. Mark" (Donatello), 88–89, 90, Plate III

St. Thomas Aquinas, 71, 150

Salutati, Coluccio, 42, 43, 44

Sannazaro, Jacopo, 60

Sarbiewski, Casimir, 60

Savonarola, Girolamo, 122

Seay, Albert, 165 n. 4, 167 n. 26, 168 n. 33

Secundus, Johannes, 60

Seneca, 22, 57, 72

Shakespeare, William, 11, 20–21, 24, 54, 58, 69, 73–74, 75

Shelton, Thomas, as translator of *Don Quixote*, 62

Shepherd's Calendar, The (Spenser), 66

Sidney, Sir Philip, 23, 57, 68

Skelton, John, 21

Socrates, 22, 39

Soderini, Francesco, 93

Sophocles, 59

Spataro, Giovanni, 158, 176 n. 99

Spenser, Edmund, 9, 21, 65, 66–68, 70; *see also Faerie Queene, The; Shepherd's Calendar, The*
Spingarn, Joel E., 68
Stella Maris; see John of Garland
Strabo, 118
Strozzi, Palla, 107
Sylvester, Josuah, 62

Table Talks; see Intercænales
Tansillo, Luigi, 47
Tasso, Torquato, 67, 68
Telesio, Bernardino, 40
Theocritus, 66
Theorica musicae, 150–51; *see also* Gafori, Franchino
Thorndike, Lynn, 106
Timotheus, 152
Tinctoris, Johannes, 130, 132–33, 134, 135–36, 137–45, 148–51, 155, 157, 161–63; *see also Complexus effectuum musices; De arte contrapuncti; Proportionale*
Toscanelli, Paolo dal Pozzo, 6, 105–27
"Trajanus Decius," 92
Traversari, Ambrogio, 107
Trilling, Lionel, 62
Tyndale, William, 63

Uccello, Paolo, 108
Urquhart, Sir Thomas, 62

Utopia (More), 61
Uzielli, 106
Uzzano, Niccolò da, 107

Valla, Lorenzo, 56
Vasari, Giorgio, 37, 78
Venus, 121–22
"Venus" (Pisano), 84
"Venus," Lysippean, 81–82, 94
Vesalius, Andreas, 33, 170 n. 53
Vicentino, Nicola, 130, 148, 160–61
Vida, Marco Girolamo, 60
Virgil, 66, 67, 119, 120, 121, 150, 155, 156
"Virtue" (Pisano), 82, Plate I
Visconti, Giangaleazzo, 77, 87
Vives, Juan Luis, 33
Voltaire, François Marie, 65, 126

Walker, D. P., 172 n. 62
Weinmann, Karl, 167 n. 30
Willaert, Adrian, 146, 171 n. 53, 176 n. 99

Zabarella, Francesco, 34
Zarlino, Gioseffo, da Chioza, 130, 138, 146, 147–48, 160–61
Zoroaster, 39
"Zuccone" (Donatello), 91–92, Plates VII, X